WHEN CHRIST WAS HERE A WOMEN'S BIBLE STUDY

CLAUDIA BARBA

journeyforth®

Greenville, South Carolina

Elisabeth Elliot, *Keep a Quiet Heart* (Ann Arbor, MI: Vine Books, 1995), 25.

"The Incarnation of the Triune God," December 21, 1980 and 2003 (http://www.gty.org/resources/sermons/2003/the-incarnation-of-the-triune-god#top).

Matthew Henry, *An Exposition of All the Books of the Old and New Testaments*, Volume 4 (London: W. Baynes, 1806), 595.

Elisabeth Elliot, *A Lamp For My Feet* (Ann Arbor, MI: Servant Publications, 1985), 83.

G. Campbell Morgan, *The Crises of the Christ* (London: Fleming H. Revell Company, 1903), 157, 183.

Cover Photo Credits: istockphoto/OGphoto

All Scripture is quoted from the Authorized King James Version.

When Christ Was Here: A Women's Bible Study
Claudia Barba

Design and page layout by Nathan Hutcheon

© 2011 BJU Press
Greenville, South Carolina 29614
JourneyForth Books is a division of BJU Press.

Printed in the United States of America

ISBN 978-1-60682-162-6

15   14   13   12   11   10   9   8   7   6   5   4   3

CONTENTS

INTRODUCTION

A rectangular stone, about three feet long and crowned with an oval-shaped depression, sat in the corner of a museum of biblical antiquities. Curious, I checked the museum guidebook and discovered to my surprise that the odd stone was a manger recovered from the ruins of an inn in Bethlehem.

I stood staring at it for a long time, transfixed by the thought that the God of the universe could—that He would—come to earth to lie as a helpless newborn on a stone of His own creation! Though that day in the museum was long ago, I've never gotten over the wonder of it. The story of the incarnation of Jesus Christ still amazes me and inspires my praise.

Was that manger *the* manger? I doubt it. My instincts tell me that the Lord has not allowed such relics to be preserved, for then we would be tempted to worship the symbol rather than the Savior. We don't need to see and touch relics to believe. We need faith instead. Physical objects do not matter, but His coming to live among us does. In fact, His coming "in the flesh" makes all the difference!

Because He came, we can be saved. Because He came, we can see the invisible God. Because He came, we have a High Priest, Who sympathizes with our flawed humanity. And because He came, we have a faultless example for earthly living.

Let the lessons that follow help you appreciate the truth of the incarnation and apply this truth to your life.

At the very beginning of our study, it's important to understand what the incarnation is and what it means, for at the core of almost every false religion is an open denial or some sort of distortion of this doctrine. If you know what you believe, and are certain that your belief is firmly based in Scripture, you won't be easily fooled by false teachers.

Our family has come to know a man who is a committed unbeliever. He is an intelligent inquirer, though, and curious about what we believe. When the subject of the incarnation came up in conversation, he declared, "I don't believe that!" When asked why, he responded without hesitation, "Because it's impossible!" And that is of course the whole point, isn't it? It is incomprehensible to any natural mind that Jesus could be that absolutely unique Person Who was at once both God and man. But what seems impossible to a human can still be true, for God is not limited by man's understanding. He can do the impossible. Our task is not to figure out how He does it but to accept by faith that what He says is true.

> The mystery of the humanity of Christ, that He sunk Himself into our flesh, is beyond all human understanding.
>
> *–Martin Luther*

PROMISED BEFORE HIS COMING

1. There's a special name at the end of Isaiah 7:14—a name to be given to the virgin-born Messiah. What is it?

Immanuel

In Matthew 1:23, an angel quoted this prophecy when he

explained Jesus' imminent birth to Joseph. What did he say the name meant?

God with us

What an astonishing prophecy! God—the holy, eternal, all-powerful One—was coming to earth to be with His creatures. In a prophecy of His birth, He was also given some other remarkable names: "For unto us a child is born, unto us a son is given: and the government shall be upon his shoulder: and his name shall be called Wonderful, Counsellor, the mighty God, the everlasting Father, the Prince of Peace" (Isaiah 9:6).

2. Circle the two names in the above verse that most clearly declare Christ's deity.

Micah 5:2 is well-known for its prediction that the birth of the Messiah would take place in the "little town of Bethlehem" in Judah. What does this verse teach about the Messiah, the "ruler in Israel" *before* His birth?

from ancient of days

3. When the angel Gabriel talked with the virgin Mary about her conceiving a child, he said that all three members of the Trinity would be present at that moment. List them from Luke 1:35.

Holy Spirit, Most High, Son of God

BELIEVED AFTER HIS COMING
The Testimony of John

4. What four important things does John tell us about "the word" in John 1:1–3?

• it was in the beginning

· with God   · was God

· in the beginning with God

5. Answer these questions from John 1:14. In what form did the Word come?

flesh

Where did He live?

among sinners

When men saw the Word, Whom were they seeing?

Jesus

Jesus' life was different from the life of every other person in this way: it began long before He was conceived. His birth was His coming, not His beginning, for He has existed from eternity. John used an interesting word for "dwell" in John 1:14—one that says literally that Jesus "tabernacled" with us. Though the Old Testament tabernacle was just a tent, it was a sacred place, "the tabernacle of the congregation [of meeting]" (Exodus 33:7–11), where the children of Israel met directly with God. This encounter took place just once a year, with intricate ceremony, and only through their representative, the high priest. Jesus, the God-man, however, tabernacled among us in a much more personal and accessible way.

John the apostle was one of Jesus' closest friends. He ate, drank, and traveled with the Savior, an eyewitness to His ministry, miracles, death, and resurrection. He wrote the book of 1 John partly to refute the heresy of the deniers of the incarnation.

6. Read the first two verses of 1 John. What phrase in verse 2 teaches Christ's deity?

He was in the beginning with God

The Testimony of Paul

The apostle Paul confirms what John taught. Jesus was born to a virgin—which is certainly not normal—but otherwise He was born through natural human processes "according to the flesh."

7. Read Romans 1:3–4. What event proved beyond doubt that this otherwise ordinary man was "the Son of God with power"?

_____

Paul spends much of the next seven chapters convincing the Romans of the terrible weakness of their flesh—of their total inability to save themselves by keeping the Old Testament law. Just as their case seems most hopeless, he reminds them of their great hope of salvation—the incarnation!

> For the law of the Spirit of life in Christ Jesus hath made me free from the law of sin and death. For what the law could not do, in that it was weak through the flesh, God sending his own Son in the likeness of sinful flesh, and for sin, condemned sin in the flesh. (Romans 8:3)

8. What did the "law of the spirit of life in Christ Jesus" do that the old law could never do (Romans 8:2)?

_____

"In the likeness of" is an important phrase! Jesus was not a sinner, but He appeared in the likeness—the shape or form—of a sinful human.

When Jesus lived a sinless life and then died "for sin," He fulfilled all the law's demands and destroyed its authority over all who accept Him as Savior. Think about the hundreds of laws recorded in the first five books of the Old Testament. How would your life be different if you were required to keep all of them? Praise Jesus for the incarnation, for it means that the law has no power to condemn you!

In his letter to the church at Philippi, Paul beautifully describes the incarnation of Christ as he encourages his friends to be like Him.

> Let this mind [this disposition; this way of thinking] be in you, which was also in Christ Jesus: who, being in the form [the essential nature, the substance] of God, thought it not robbery [something to be held onto] to be equal with God: but made himself of no reputation, and took upon him the form [the essential nature, the substance] of a servant, and was made in the likeness [only in appearance] of men. And being found in fashion [in external appearance] as a man, he humbled himself, and became obedient unto death, even the death of the cross. Wherefore God also hath highly exalted him, and given him a name which is above every name: that at the name of Jesus every knee should bow, of things in heaven, and things in earth, and things under the earth, and that every tongue should confess that Jesus Christ is Lord, to the glory of God the Father. (Philippians 2:5–11)

9. Which two phrases in verse 6 indicate that Jesus was deity?

_____

The Greek word used for "equal" in verse 6 means "to be exactly the same in every way"—not just in shape, size, or quantity but also in quality and character. We can accurately say, based on this verse, that Jesus Christ = God. Jesus took on the essential nature of a servant (*doulos*: a bond slave) and assumed the outward likeness of a man (Philippians 2:7). But He did even more for you.

10. How low did He go (verse 8)?

_____

When Jesus "made himself of no reputation," He emptied Himself—not of His deity but of the manifestation of His glory as God. He sacrificed the riches and delights of heaven for the poverty and trials of earth: "For ye know the grace of our Lord Jesus Christ, that, though he was rich, yet for your sakes he became poor, that ye through his poverty might be rich" (2 Corinthians 8:9). He surrendered His right to be honored, allowing Himself instead to be "despised and rejected of men" (Isaiah 53:3). During His hours on the cross, carrying "our sins in his own body" (1 Peter 2:24), He even sacrificed fellowship with His Father: "My God, my God, why hast thou forsaken me?" (Mark 15:34).

> 11. Because of His willing humiliation, what has the Father done—and what will He do—for the Son (Philippians 2:9–11)?

Though today many deny His deity or try simply to ignore Him, someday all angels and demons, along with all humans who have ever been born, will bow before Him in worship as He is declared King of Kings and Lord of Lords (Revelation 19:19). It's our privilege to joyfully and willingly do this right now!

Paul wrote 1 Timothy to a young pastor who needed both practical advice and doctrinal instruction. First Timothy 3:16 is summarizes the truth that Paul calls the great "mystery of godliness." It's not the kind of mystery Sherlock Holmes could solve but instead is truth that was hidden in Old Testament times and revealed in New Testament days.

> 12. What six facts from 1 Timothy 3:16 make up this now-revealed mystery? (These are events of Jesus' earthly history—from His birth to His ministry to His ascension.)

_____

_____

_____

_____

The second half of verse 16 is lines from a poem, quoted from a hymn of the early church. Just as today, believers in those days learned much of their doctrine from the songs they sang. Christians still celebrate the incarnation in song—such as in these lines from a familiar Christmas carol:

> *Veiled in flesh, the Godhead see.*
> *Hail, the incarnate deity!*
> *Hark, the herald angels sing,*
> *Glory to the newborn King!*

As you sing hymns, listen for phrases that teach the truth of the incarnation.

13. Read Colossians 1:12–18. This is another of Paul's letters. Who is the "whom" of verse 14?

_____

_____

What two phrases describe Him in verse 15?

_____

_____

_____

When as a child I met a very old great-uncle for the first time, he told me in his creaky-squeaky voice that I was the spittin' image of my father. Of course I wasn't an exact replica—I was much shorter and had more hair! Jesus Christ, however, is much more than an approximate facsimile of God. He is the precise, perfect likeness of His Father, reflecting and revealing Him in every way.

7

14. What did Jesus do that only God has power to do (Colossians 1:16)?

_____

"All things were made by him; and without him was not anything made that was made" (John 1:3). What is He now doing in creation that only God can do (Colossians 1:17)?

_____

Jesus, Who is always the same (Hebrews 13:8), is now and always has been the Creator and Sustainer of all. He spoke the worlds into existence and holds together all the molecules of all He created. As He walked on earth under the light of the sun and stars, He maintained their orbits. While living in a limited region of a small planet, He governed a world of inconceivable scope—a universe He engineered. He subjected Himself to the natural laws that He wrote, while, as Elisabeth Elliot said, "choreograph[ing] the molecular dance which goes on every second of every minute of every day in every cell in the universe."

As He carried water for His mother, He preserved its bonds of hydrogen and oxygen. He was the Maker of the wood in Joseph's carpenter shop and of the timber of His own cross. The metal of nails and spear was of His design, and as wicked men wielded them as weapons against Him, He was sustaining the muscles, nerves, and bones that made their assaults possible. Though He was "before all things, and by him all things consist," yet in His humility, He allowed Himself to be abused by His creatures.

15. What position does He hold that no mere human can hold (Colossians 1:18)?

_____

What does the phrase "the firstborn from the dead" reveal about Jesus?

_____

God, who at sundry times and in divers manners spake in time past unto the fathers by the prophets, hath in these last days spoken unto us by his Son, whom he hath appointed heir of all things, by whom also he made the worlds; who being the brightness of his glory, and the express image of his person, and upholding all things by the word of his power, when he had by himself purged our sins, sat down on the right hand of the Majesty on high. (Hebrews 1:1–3)

16. What has God the Father done through His Son?

_____

What does Jesus reveal about His Father?

_____

What is Jesus' relationship to nature?

_____

What did He do for us?

_____

Where is He now?

_____

"In all things," in all earth and heaven, Jesus, the God-man, has been given preeminence by His Father. He is supreme—creator and sustainer, redeemer and intercessor, God in the flesh, and God with you.

17. Have you given Him preeminence on this day?

_____

What place has He had in your schedule?

_____

How many of your thoughts have been of your Savior?

_____

Have you told others about Him?

_____

How have you used your abilities and your resources to serve Him?

_____

How have you crowned Him Lord of this day?

_____

There's no doubt that the New Testament writers, the men who knew Him best, believed that Jesus was God in the flesh. Do you? Does it make any difference? Some people would say that it doesn't matter—that the incarnation is an optional doctrine—for Jesus was certainly a good man and remarkable teacher even if He was not God. But the Bible makes it clear that this is an essential doctrine.

18. Read 1 John 4:1–4. A true teacher, one with the "Spirit of God," believes and teaches that Jesus Christ was fully human and fully divine. How can you identify someone who has the "spirit of antichrist"?

_____

_____

19. John's warnings are even stronger in 2:22–23. What labels does he apply to those who deny the deity of Christ?

_____

What does he call them in 2 John 7?

_____

20. Can you be a Christian without believing that Jesus is God (1 John 2:23; 2 John 9)?

_____

21. When a representative of any religion knocks on your door, hoping to make a convert of you, what is the first question you should ask?

_____

22. How should you respond to someone who comes to teach you spiritual things but does not believe this doctrine (2 John 10)?

_____

Why (2 John 11)?

_____

Obviously, the incarnation matters! It's a vital, foundational doctrine, and it is crucial for you to believe it and be able to defend it.

> The affirmation of the deity of Jesus Christ is the *sine qua non* [indispensable element] of all that we believe. That is why it is always under attack. It is the deity of Jesus Christ that is the substantive affirmation of the Christian faith.
>
> *—John MacArthur*

And the word was made flesh, and dwelt among us, and we beheld his glory, the glory as of the only begotten of the Father, full of grace and truth. (John 1:14)

Jesus Christ was "self-conscious" in the very best way. People who listened carefully to Him knew that He was presenting Himself as the Messiah—the only begotten Son of God. Some believed, followed, and worshiped Him. Those who did not believe crucified Him instead. These were opposite reactions to Jesus' unmistakable declarations and demonstrations that He was God.

If He was not God, He was not even good. What would you think of a human, no matter how virtuous, who allowed himself be worshiped as God? How would you feel about an ordinary man who claimed power to forgive sins? Who asked his followers to abandon everything to follow him? Who claimed that someday he would judge the world? If Jesus was not God, He was a charlatan, a fraud, an imposter—or a madman. He cannot be good without being God. In fact, if He is not God, He is one of the worst of men.

As you study this lesson from the Gospels, you'll understand that your faith in Jesus' deity has a solid foundation in His own words and actions. He was more than just good; He was perfect. And without a doubt, He knew that He was God!

JESUS' WORDS

He Claimed to Be Messiah—the Anointed One

Jesus had an interesting conversation with the disciples in Caesarea Philippi. You will find it recorded in Matthew 16:13–17.

1. When He asked His disciples who others thought He was, what did they answer?

_____

But then Jesus asked a more direct question: "But whom say

13

ye that I am?" Peter, the outspoken disciple, declared, "Thou art the Christ, the Son of the living God!"

- "Christ" = the Messiah, the Anointed One promised by the prophets
- "the Son" = the second member of the Trinity
- "of the living God" = of the one true God Jehovah, the Source of all life

2. These were more than just words; they were the confident cry of Peter's believing heart. If Jesus had been only a good man Who knew that He was not God, how do you think He would have responded to His close friend and disciple Peter?

_____

But instead, Jesus praised him! What did He say in verse 17 to assure Peter that he had spoken truth?

_____

In the next verse Jesus emphasized the importance of Peter's confession of faith, labeling his words as the foundational doctrine of His church.

> And I say also unto thee, That thou art Peter [*petros*, a small stone], and upon this rock [*petra*, a foundation stone] I will build my church; and the gates of hell shall not prevail against it.

He Claimed Equality with God—One with the Father

Another exchange between Master and disciples is found in John 14:1–7. Jesus told the disciples that He was going away to prepare a place for them. Practical Thomas wanted to know how to get there. In answer, Jesus made this classic statement about Himself:

> Jesus saith unto him, I am the way, the truth, and the life: no man cometh unto the Father, but by me. If ye had known me, ye should have

known my Father also: and from henceforth ye know him, and have seen him. (John 14:6–7)

3. Are these claims that any other sane, honest man could make about himself? Explain.

_____

What did Jesus want Thomas to know?

_____

4. Philip then asked to be shown the Father (verse 8). How did Jesus respond (verses 9–11)?

_____

5. What did Jesus do and say in John 5:18 that made the Jews angry enough to want to kill Him?

_____

In the following verse, Jesus explained that He could "do nothing of himself" apart from the Father. He was not saying that He did not have adequate power alone but that because of their essential union, He could not act independently of His Father.

> In all things he must, from the necessity of his nature, act in accordance with the nature and will of God. . . . There is no separate action—no separate existence; but, alike in being and in action, there is the most perfect oneness between him and the Father.
>
> *—Albert Barnes*

He Claimed to Be Eternal—He Has Always Existed

Another of Jesus' exchanges with leading Jews is recorded in John 8. When He said, "If a man keep my saying, he shall never see death" (verse 52), they replied angrily that He had a demon. When He said, "Before Abraham was, I am" (verse 58), they picked up rocks to stone Him! By naming Himself "I AM," He was undoubtedly identifying Himself as the eternal, unchanging, self-existent God, Who had told Moses that His name was "I AM WHO I AM" (Exodus 3:13–14). The Jews understood that Jesus was declaring Himself to be Jehovah. Stoning was the punishment for what they considered to be blasphemy (Leviticus 24:16).

6. As Jesus prayed to His Father not long before the crucifixion, how did He again declare that He is eternal (John 17:5, 24)?

JESUS' ACTIONS

Even while living on earth in a human body, Jesus did what only God could do.

Jesus Was Omnipotent—He Had All Power

7. The following verses show His power over what?

Matthew 8:1–3; Luke 4:38–40

Matthew 8:16, 28–32; Luke 4:33–36

Matthew 8:23–27

Luke 7:11–16; 8:49–56

Jesus Was Omniscient—He Knew All Things

When Jesus first met Nathanael, He said that He had already "seen" him praying, or meditating, under the shade of a fig tree.

Since Jesus could not have physically seen him, Jesus' knowledge of his devotional habits had to have been supernatural.

8. Read John 1:45–51. How did Nathanael respond to this realization (verse 49)?

_____

During the conversation with the Samaritan woman recorded in John 4, Jesus revealed that He knew all about her past (verses 16–18) though He had never met her. Then He declared plainly that He is the Messiah, the Christ (verses 25–26).

9. What did the Samaritan woman conclude about Him? Why (verses 28–29)?

_____

_____

_____

10. In the following Scriptures, what did Jesus know that only God can know?

Matthew 12:24–25

_____

Luke 5:21–22

_____

Luke 6:7–8

_____

11. Read Luke 7:36–50. To whom was the Pharisee Simon speaking in verse 39?

_____

Verse 40 says that Jesus "answering said unto him." What does that reveal about Jesus?

_____

12. According to John 6:70–71 and 13:11, 21, what terrible event did Jesus know before it happened?

_____

Jesus Had Authority—He Forgave Sins

Jesus' deity was proved in the wonderful story recorded in Mark 2 of the paralytic lowered through roof tiles to Jesus' feet. The disabled man's friends knew he needed physical healing, but Jesus knew his deeper need: forgiveness of sin. When He announced, "Son, thy sins be forgiven thee," the scribes were furious (verses 6–7) but didn't make their disbelief public.

13. How did Jesus know about their attitude (verse 8)?

_____

The scribes were right about one thing—only God can forgive sins. But they were wrong to label Jesus a blasphemer. He was not pretending to be God; He is God. One of the reasons He performed this miracle of healing was that all would know that "the Son of man hath power on earth to forgive sins" (Matthew 9:6).

The scribes were unwilling to accept the irrefutable evidence of His deity that was right before their eyes. Jesus had instantly reversed severe paralysis and accurately read private thoughts. These miracles established His authority to forgive sins, for they proved Him to be God. The God Who heals is the God Who can forgive.

> Bless the Lord, O my soul, and forget not all his benefits: who forgiveth all thine iniquities; who healeth all thy diseases. (Psalm 103:2–3)
>
> To the Lord our God belong mercies and forgivenesses. (Daniel 9:9)

18

Behold one of the great Physician's mightiest arts: He has power to forgive sin! While here He lived below, before the ransom had been paid, before the blood had been literally sprinkled on the mercy-seat, He had power to forgive sin. Hath He not power to do it now that He hath died? What power must dwell in Him who to the utmost farthing has faithfully discharged the debts of His people! He has boundless power now that He has finished transgression and made an end of sin. If ye doubt it, see Him rising from the dead! Behold Him in ascending splendor raised to the right hand of God! Hear Him pleading before the eternal Father, pointing to His wounds, urging the merit of His sacred passion! What power to forgive is here!

–Charles H. Spurgeon

Jesus Accepted Worship—He Deserved It

Even before His birth, Jesus' mother's cousin Elisabeth praised Him and called Him Lord.

> And she spake out with a loud voice, and said, Blessed art thou among women, and blessed is the fruit of thy womb. And whence is this to me, that the mother of my Lord should come to me? (Luke 1:42–43)

14. When the angel of the Lord appeared to the shepherds in the field to announce Jesus' birth, what name did he give Him (Luke 2:10–11)?

_____

Later in Luke 2:25–39, Simeon and Anna recognized Jesus, only eight days old, as the Messiah—"the consolation of Israel," "the Lord's Christ," and "[God's] salvation." Later the wise men also worshiped the young child Jesus and gave Him gifts worthy of a king.

> And when they were come into the house, they saw the young child with Mary his mother, and fell down, and worshipped him: and when they

19

had opened their treasures, they presented unto him gifts; gold, and frankincense, and myrrh. (Matthew 2:11)

It's exciting to recognize in the wise men's worship a fulfillment of the prophecy of Psalm 72:10: "The kings of Tarshish and of the isles shall bring presents: the kings of Sheba and Seba shall offer gifts." Although this psalm refers primarily to King Solomon, it is full of predictions about the Messiah. Compare Psalm 72:11, "Yea, all kings shall fall down before him: all nations shall serve him," to Philippians 2:10–11. This baby Jesus was no ordinary child!

As He grew into manhood and began His ministry, others who recognized Him as the Messiah also worshiped Him. John 9 tells a remarkable story of the healing of a man born blind. The unbelieving Pharisees, determined to disprove Jesus' claim to be Messiah, interrogated the former beggar. "What sayest thou of him, that he hath opened thine eyes?" they demanded.

15. Who did the healed man say Jesus was when they questioned him (verse 17)?

_____

When Jesus met with the man later, He asked, "Dost thou believe on the Son of God?" The former beggar responded simply, "Who is he, Lord, that I may believe in him?" What was Jesus' answer (verse 37)?

_____

What could be more straightforward? Jesus identified Himself as the Son of God and accepted the worship of this new believer (verse 38).

The disciples came to a gradual understanding of Jesus' deity as they watched Him walk on water, feed two huge crowds by multiplying food, and heal suffering multitudes. While still in the boat after He calmed a Galilee storm, these men of little faith expressed their growing comprehension when they "worshipped him, saying, Of a truth thou art the Son of God" (Matthew 14:33).

Jesus did not correct them. He accepted their worship.

Even after the resurrection, Thomas doubted. "Except I shall see in his hands the print of the nails, and put my finger into the print of the nails, and thrust my hand into his side, I will not believe" (John 20:25). But the resurrected Christ, Who understood Thomas's pessimistic temperament, appeared and offered His wounded hands and side for Thomas to touch. "Be not faithless," He encouraged him, "but believing" (verse 27). And Thomas did believe! With absolute certainty, he then identified his Master.

16. What did he call Jesus (verse 28)?

_____

Jesus praised Thomas and accepted his worship, for as God, He deserved it! Then in verse 29, Jesus praised you! "Blessed are they that have not seen and yet have believed."

Do you believe in the incarnation? Those who believe by faith, without seeing, are blessed! And if you believe, then you will worship Jesus Christ as God, just as Thomas did.

> And we believe and are sure that thou art that
> Christ, the Son of the living God. (John 6:69)

Jesus was not only God; He was God incarnate—in flesh. Through the means of His virgin birth, the eternal Son of God took on an additional nature that was fully human but without sin. "And ye know that he was manifested [became visible] to take away our sins; and in him is no sin" (1 John 3:5). The sinless One appeared in human form, and because He did, He can be our Savior.

The doctrine of the humanity of Jesus Christ has a clear foundation in Hebrews 2:14—"Forasmuch then as the children are partakers of flesh and blood he also himself likewise took part of the same; that through death he might destroy him that had the power of death, that is, the devil."

Since people have flesh and blood, He took on a human nature, also with flesh and blood, so that through His death, He could destroy the Devil's power over humanity. Hebrews 9:26 says, "Now once in the end of the world hath he appeared to put away sin by the sacrifice of himself."

Still some doubt that God came in human flesh. As early as the first century, a group known as the Gnostics taught that matter is always evil and spirit is always good. Therefore, they declared, since Jesus was a divine Being, He could not have possessed a physical body. He only appeared to be human. Another false teacher of the period taught that from His baptism until His crucifixion, the divine spirit of Christ simply inhabited the body of a man named Jesus.

THE IMPORTANCE OF HIS HUMANITY

Does His humanity matter? Discover in these Scriptures why it was essential for Christ to possess both divine and human natures.

1. According to Hebrews 9:22, what is necessary for forgiveness ("remission") of sin?

_____

Jesus had to have a human body to be able to meet this requirement.

2. Read Exodus 12:5; Leviticus 22:19–21; and 23:12. What was essential in every sacrifice?

_____

3. According to 1 Peter 1:19, why was Jesus, the "Lamb of God," a worthy sacrifice?

_____

Because Jesus was human, He could shed blood. Because He was God, His perfect blood could atone for our sins.

> For he hath made him to be sin for us, who knew no sin; that we might be made the righteousness of God in him. (2 Corinthians 5:21)

> We are sanctified through the offering of the body of Jesus Christ once for all. (Hebrews 10:10)

THE PROOF OF HIS HUMANITY

During the second half of the first century, the aging apostle John wrote the letter we know as 1 John. He was the sole surviving apostle—the only one still alive of the close, personal observers of Jesus' earthly life. Stories about Jesus were not just hearsay to John; they were part of his personal life history. As an eyewitness he had both authority and credibility among the early believers. When the Gnostics began spreading false doctrine in the churches, John took action to combat their dangerous heresy. In unambiguous words, he reminded the believers that Jesus was both God and God in flesh.

He didn't waste time with polite greetings at the beginning of 1 John but moved quickly to his theme. Read 1 John 1:1 aloud, substituting the name "Jesus" for every "which."

4. Which three physical senses does John appeal to in making his case?

_____

_____

_____

A spirit perhaps may be seen or even heard, but it cannot be handled or touched. In verses 2–3, John builds his argument by repeating his experiences as an eyewitness. Sixty years earlier, John and the other apostles had heard Jesus' voice, seen Him up close, and touched His body. However, the false teachers—the deniers of the incarnation—had never seen Him. With the authority of personal experience, John declared what He knew to be true: the eternal Word Who was once "with the Father . . . was manifested [made visible] unto us." The testimony of an eyewitness carries great weight. The body of Jesus Christ, John the eyewitness says, was undeniably human.

THE STAGES OF HIS HUMANITY

Jesus the Infant

After the amazing miracle of His conception, Jesus was carried in Mary's womb through a normal span of pregnancy and delivered through womanly labor just as any child would be. Mary "brought forth her firstborn son, and wrapped him in swaddling clothes, and laid him in a manger" (Luke 2:7). Think about the idealized nativity scenes you see displayed at Christmas. Don't you suspect that on that first Christmas morning, considering that she had just given birth, Mary and her baby might have looked just a little different from those statues? Jesus would have appeared as a typical newborn, and Mary would probably have looked exhausted from the journey to Bethlehem and her labor. Her glow would have come from joy at the safe delivery of her firstborn—not from a halo hovering over her head. But nativity scenes do serve as a visible reminder of this astounding fact: on a day long ago, God came down to earth in the form of a baby laid in a manger. This unique baby was held in the gentle arms of two who looked on Him with the loving wonder of all new parents and with the angel-revealed knowledge that this baby was the virgin-born Son of God.

Jesus the Adult

Jesus lived for more than thirty years as an ordinary unmarried citizen of His community. Think about His daily life during those years. What tasks would have been part of His routine? Does anything in your daily schedule look similar to His?

When this extraordinary God-man first publicly claimed to be the Messiah in His hometown synagogue, His neighbors reacted strongly (Matthew 13:54–57).

5. How does Matthew describe their reactions (verses 54, 57)?

_____

What two specific things amazed them (verse 54)?

_____

I'm not sure how it's possible to be sinless and not be noticed, but for thirty years His townspeople had apparently detected nothing about Him that would distinguish Him from other men. Maybe all they remembered was that He had once gotten lost during a family trek to Jerusalem. He lived and worked in an unpretentious way, in a family setting, for about 90 percent of His time on earth.

Most of us live as He did, among the great crowd of common people. Lacking colossal wealth or remarkable talent, without celebrity or power, the best most of us can be is average. We are ordinary people living ordinary lives. It's encouraging to remember that Jesus, God incarnate, was placed among us. Because He lived where we live, He can understand our simple daily needs and struggles. He identifies with us regular folks. While teaching, Jesus drew on His life as a human to shine light on truth, using illustrations drawn from familiar activities like sweeping (Luke 15:8–10) and baking bread (Matthew 13:33).

We don't know exactly how Jesus looked, because no authentic drawings or paintings of Him exist. We have a clue to His appearance, though, in John 4:9.

6. How do you think the Samaritan woman at the well would have known at their first meeting that Jesus was Jewish?

_____

_____

THE EXPERIENCES OF HIS HUMANITY

7. What physical needs and limitations of Jesus do these Scriptures reveal?

Matthew 4:2; 21:18

_____

Matthew 8:24

_____

John 4:6

_____

John 4:7; 19:28

_____

27

8. What human emotions did He experience?

Matthew 9:36

_____

Matthew 26:38

_____

John 12:27

_____

John 13:34

_____

9. What did Jesus learn (Hebrews 5:8)?

_____

Jesus obeyed His earthly parents, but His ultimate obedience was to the will of His Father in heaven. He said in John 6:38, "For I came down from heaven, not to do mine own will, but the will of him that sent me." Philippians 2:8 reminds us that His obedience extended "unto death, even the death of the cross."

THE BLESSINGS OF HIS HUMANITY

Because Jesus was incarnated, we can see the invisible God. "No man hath seen God at any time; the only begotten Son . . . he hath declared him" (John 1:18). The Son's incarnation has made it possible for us, with our literal minds more accustomed to the concrete than the abstract, to see an otherwise unseeable God. As we follow Jesus' footsteps on earth, we come to understand the character of God.

10. What can we learn about the Father from the words and deeds of His Son in the following verses?

Matthew 15:32

Matthew 20:30–34

Mark 10:17–22

Luke 19:41

John 2:15

Because Jesus was incarnated, we have an Intercessor Who understands. A little boy in his bed became frightened and called to his daddy, "It's dark up here and I'm scared!" His father replied, "Don't be afraid. God is there with you." In a few minutes the boy called louder, "Daddy, come; I need somebody with skin on!" Because Jesus has been here, "with skin on," He understands what it's like to be human.

> For we have not an high priest which cannot be touched [sympathize] with the feeling of our infirmities [weaknesses], but was in all points tempted like as we are, yet without sin. (Hebrews 4:15)

He knows how to give help and relief when we are attacked.

> For in that he himself hath suffered being tempted, he is able to succour them that are tempted. (Hebrews 2:18)

Once when my husband and I were in the middle of an especially painful trial, a friend called us just to say, "I have been right where you are, and I know exactly how you feel." Those simple words were an immeasurable comfort—exactly what we needed to hear. No matter what your trial, the Son of God, Who was tested in every way exactly as you are, can say to you, "I have been right where you are, and I know exactly how you feel." The huge difference is this: though our friend understood, loved, and comforted us, he was powerless to end our trial. Jesus Christ not only understands, loves, and comforts, He also has power to change your circumstances!

11. When you're in a trial, what does He do (Hebrews 7:24–25; Romans 8:34)?

12. When you fail and give in to temptation, then what does He do?

1 Timothy 2:5

1 John 1:9

What a wonderful Friend! He has been here, so He understands what it's like to be surrounded by flesh. When you want to do right with your mind but your flesh makes it a struggle, He understands—because of the incarnation!

> For I delight in the law of God after the inward man: but I see another law in my members, warring against the law of my mind, and bringing me into captivity to the law of sin which is in my members. O wretched man that I am! who shall deliver me from the body of this death? I thank God through Jesus Christ our Lord. (Romans 7:22–25)

Because Jesus was incarnated, we have an example for earthly living. Jesus could have come to earth for a short time—days, weeks, months—perfectly fulfilled the law and then died and been resurrected. But instead He lived here, walking on the earth, for about thirty-three years, to set an example of how to live as a human and how to deal with a variety of other people. In the following lessons, you will discover the pattern that Jesus set for earthly living. You need to know how He lived on earth because you are commanded to live as He lived.

> He that saith he abideth in him ought himself
> also so to walk, even as he walked. (1 John 2:6)

LESSON 4

Family members can be our best friends or our worst enemies. They may even—to our chagrin—be both at the same time! Jesus understands that relationships with family members can be difficult. Nothing you can tell Him about your family will surprise Him, for He, too, once belonged to a human family. For thirty years, as He lived in the Nazareth home of Mary and Joseph, He experienced the strength of family ties and the pain of family rejection.

FAMILY MEMBERS

1. According to Matthew 13:55–56, who were Jesus' four half-brothers?

_____

_____

   Mary was their mother, but God Himself, rather than Joseph, was Jesus' Father. Jesus also had at least how many half-sisters? So at least how many children lived in Jesus' home?

_____

2. Jesus also had extended family members. The Bible names some of them (Luke 1:36, 57–60; John 19:25). List them.

_____

_____

_____

Mary

Soon after the angel announced to the young virgin Mary that she was to bear the Messiah, she visited her cousin Elisabeth, who, though well past normal childbearing years, was pregnant through God's miraculous intervention. After an encouraging greeting from Elisabeth, Mary prayed a remarkable prayer, recorded in Luke 1:46–55. It's often called her Magnificat for the Latin translation of the opening words "My soul doth magnify." Her extemporaneous prayer is packed with references to the Pentateuch, the Old Testament books of history, Job, Psalms, and the prophets. She quoted freely from them and showed understanding of their meaning.

3. What does her knowledge of the Old Testament reveal about Mary?

What was her relationship to Jehovah?

4. In Luke 1:38, she had responded to the angel's remarkable announcement by calling herself what?

In verse 48, she used the same word, which can mean either a voluntary or involuntary bond slave. Which do you think Mary was?

5. Some falsely teach that Mary herself was sinless from birth through her "immaculate conception." How do you know this is not true (verse 47)?

6. What do we learn about the disposition of Jesus' mother from Luke 2:19, 51?

_____

Joseph

The man who served God as Jesus' earthly father was a carpenter—probably an artisan who worked with stones and brick as well as with wood (Matthew 13:55). A resident of Nazareth, he had descended from "the house and lineage" of King David (Luke 2:4).

7. What character traits of Joseph are revealed in Matthew 1:18–25?

_____

_____

_____

_____

This righteous man (Matthew 1:19) also displayed courage and faith when he abandoned his home and work to flee into Egypt to protect the infant Jesus (Matthew 2:13–15).

FAMILY TRAINING

Though not a single word from Joseph is recorded in Scripture, we know that as a diligent Jewish father, he would have functioned as Jesus' example and teacher, spending a great deal of time with Him.

8. What life skills might he have modeled and taught to Jesus?

_____

The Jewish custom was to teach every male child a trade or business—usually that of the father.

9. Compare Matthew 13:55 to Mark 6:3. What trade did Jesus learn?

_____

It may seem strange to think of God the Son having to learn anything or being limited in any way. While on earth in a human body, He did not display His omniscience and omnipotence continuously—only when it was the Father's will for Him to do so. Jesus developed social, academic, and vocational skills as He experienced the full scope of human life.

10. His early years are summarized in Luke 2:40. What area of life does this verse emphasize?

_____

Nothing in our inspired Scriptures indicates that Jesus' childhood was anything other than the normal life of a Jewish child in Nazareth—with the one exception that He never did anything wrong! He would have been educated at home and then most likely in a school connected to the local synagogue. An apocryphal (uninspired) book called The Infancy Gospel of Thomas contains stories of Jesus performing capricious, self-indulgent miracles during His childhood, but we know that the sinless Savior would never have used His powers selfishly or just to show off.

11. At age twelve, He traveled to Jerusalem with His family to celebrate the Feast of the Passover (Luke 2:41–52). What do you learn about Him in verses 46–47?

_____

_____

_____

How do you think Jesus had gained such a grasp of the Scriptures by age twelve? Probably He learned in the same way as Timothy, who was reminded by his mentor, Paul, that "from a child [an infant] thou hast known the holy scriptures, which are able to make thee wise unto salvation through faith which is in Christ Jesus" (2 Timothy 3:15). Parents have a remarkable opportunity and responsibility to teach their children the Scriptures from babyhood—stories of Bible characters, life-guiding principles from Proverbs, and key doctrinal passages. Mary and Joseph must have obeyed these instructions to parents.

> And thou shalt teach them diligently unto thy children, and shalt talk of them when thou sittest in thine house, and when thou walkest by the way, and when thou liest down, and when thou risest up. (Deuteronomy 6:7)

> Shewing to the generation to come the praises of the Lord and his strength, and his wonderful works that he hath done.... That the generation to come might know them, even the children which should be born; who should arise and declare them to their children. That they might set their hope in God, and not forget the works of God, but keep his commandments. (Psalm 78:4–7)

12. What else do you learn about Jesus in Luke 2:51?

_____

In what four significant areas did He grow (verse 52)?

_____

_____

_____

FAMILY STATUS

When Jesus began to teach and preach in His own territory, those who had known Him since childhood did not deny the power of His words and deeds but were astonished that He should speak and act in the way He did (Matthew 13:54–58; Mark 6:1–6).

13. Their reactions went beyond surprise. Why were they upset and angry?

What does this tell you about the social and educational status of Jesus' immediate family?

Although Jesus' earthly family was without earthly fame, His heavenly pedigree as the Son of David is impeccable. When announcing His birth, the angel told Mary that this would be no ordinary child: "He shall be great, and shall be called the Son of the Highest: and the Lord God will give unto him the throne of his father David. And he shall reign over the house of Jacob for ever, and of his kingdom there shall be no end" (Luke 1:32–33). He was born to be King!

FAMILY REACTIONS

Misunderstanding

The first few chapters of Mark follow Jesus through busy days of demanding ministry to needy people—the demon-possessed, the diseased, the paralyzed, and the lepers. He ate with tax collectors and sinners. He debated with scribes and Pharisees. Many days He healed and spoke to multitudes all day, but still at sunset, "all the city was gathered together at the door" (Mark 1:33). "They came to him from every [direction]" (Mark 1:45) and "pressed upon him for to touch him" (Mark 3:10). They were desperate, and He was willing to help.

14. Once Jesus was so devoted to meeting people's needs that He did not take time to eat. Who came to see Him (Mark 3:21)?

The word "friends" literally means "they who were of him" and likely included His family (see verse 31). Why had they come?

_____

15. Remembering the message that the angel gave her when announcing His birth (Luke 1:35), do you think Jesus' mother Mary believed Him deranged? If not, why might she have been disturbed?

_____

This was a crucial moment for Christ. His full ministry as Messiah had begun. He had made a clear and significant statement about His priorities. As dear as His family ties were, His attachment to those who believed on Him and followed Him was even stronger.

16. Who did Jesus say are His family (Mark 3:35)? Does that include you?

_____

Rejection

John 7:1–13 records a very interesting interchange between Jesus and His half brothers. Jesus had traveled in obscure areas of Galilee, avoiding crowds. Now the time to celebrate the Feast of Tabernacles was approaching.

17. To what different region did His half brothers want Him to go for the feast?

_____

This was the popular place to be during the feast. Why did they say they wanted Him to go there?

_____

18. What does John 7:5 emphatically say about them at this point?

_____

The Lord drew a clear line between Himself and His brothers in the following verses.

19. Jesus was committed to His Father's timetable. What did He say about His time (John 7:6–8)?

_____

What did He say about their time?

_____

How did the world feel about His brothers (John 7:7)?

_____

How did the world feel about Him?

_____

Doesn't it seem strange that those who lived so closely with Jesus did not believe on Him? Even His example of perfect holiness in daily living was not enough to bring belief to their hearts. Their rejection says nothing at all about Him but everything about them.

20. Read Matthew 10:34–37. Though Jesus is the Prince of Peace, sharing His message may bring about discord—and even martyrdom (verse 39). Which family relationships may become strained after a person is converted?

_____

_____

Jesus does not encourage family conflicts, but He warns us not to be surprised when they come. The gospel always demands a response. Some will choose to believe and some will not. Those who believe will find their lives transformed in ways that cause friction—even within a loving family. Declaring allegiance to Christ may bring family disapproval, but a commitment to Him is more important than the good opinion of relatives. Earthly relationships are precious but temporary; a bond with Christ is eternal.

21. Put a check by the following that are legitimate reasons for family division after salvation?

- self-righteous or superior attitudes
- loyalty to a new Master
- isolation and lack of communication
- new convictions about standards of holy living
- a desire to please God rather than men
- an altered value system

Have you ever experienced misunderstanding or outright rejection from relatives because of your faith in Christ? Why do your goal and purposes seem so strange and disruptive to your family? How do you know Jesus understands your pain? A believer can, without compromise, maintain loving unity and friendships with unbelieving family members.

Belief

22. As Jesus suffered and died, His mother Mary stood near the cross, along with what other family member (John 19:25)?

_____

But His unbelieving half brothers apparently were not there, for to whom did Jesus commit the care of His mother (John 19:26–27)?

_____

While dying on the cross, Jesus recognized and provided for the needs of His mother (who was likely widowed by then). Even while dying on the cross, He set a pattern of loving care of parents. Caring for your aging parents is a way of serving the Lord and following His example.

23. The attitudes of at least some of His half brothers changed right away. We are not told when they were converted, but where do we find them in Acts 1:12–14?

_____

Who else was there? What were they doing?

_____

24. The conversion of Jesus' oldest half brother, James, may have been the result of an event described in 1 Corinthians 15:3–7. What wonderful privilege was James given?

_____

Later, some of Jesus' half brothers were active as itinerant missionaries. Paul mentions them and their wives in 1 Corinthians 9:5. James became the principal leader of the church at Jerusalem; he also wrote the epistle of James. Another half brother of Jesus wrote a very brief book near the end of the New Testament.

25. Refer to Matthew 13:55 and guess which brother it is.

_____

He had once refused to believe that Jesus was the Messiah. How did he describe their relationship in his book?

_____

26. The conversion of even one family member has an impact on the rest of the family. Who witnessed to his brother as soon as he became a disciple (John 1:40–42)?

_____

Who was that brother?

And just think how the Lord used him! He was the preacher on the Day of Pentecost, when about three thousand people were saved (Acts 2:14–41), and the author of 1 and 2 Peter. His testimony and writings have comforted and challenged believers for centuries—including you and me.

After his salvation, a young man named Sammy prayed, often in a barn behind his house, for his brother Bruce to be saved and delivered from his worldly lifestyle. He enlisted other family members, folks in his church, and friends around the country to pray for the brother he loved and with whom he shared a love of music. After twenty-one years, God answered those prayers, and Bruce was saved! He now travels as an evangelist. As he travels to sing and share his testimony in churches across the US, he often meets people who prayed for him to come to Christ. Close as children and now even closer as they serve the Lord together, Sammy and Bruce continue to pray for the salvation of yet another brother.

Even those family members that object most strenuously to your faith in Christ can, through your consistent example and loving testimony, come to salvation. Don't get discouraged; keep praying and witnessing, asking the Lord to open the hearts of those you love. Your changed life can change your family tree!

My husband was preaching during a week of evangelistic meetings in a large Midwestern city. He asked the church people to make special efforts to invite unsaved folks to a service when he planned to preach a clear gospel message. And they did! That evening, I stood in the church lobby and watched many visitors arrive—with earrings in places that aren't ears, with hair in colors God doesn't dye hair, with strange body odors and bizarre clothing. I saw two reactions among the regular church folks to these "invaders." Some looked shocked and dismayed, averted their eyes, and crossed quickly to the other side of the lobby, while others smiled, greeted the visitors warmly, and invited them to share their pews.

Christians today may look so good in comparison to the world that it's easy to be smugly self-righteous rather than compassionate toward the lost. In every community, couples live and raise children together, unmarried and unashamed. Some are boldly homosexual. Others publicly indulge in alcohol and drugs, curse loudly, and play raucous music that disturbs your peace. Maybe you've been scandalized as this sort of behavior has invaded your safe, comfortable enclave. You may have decided to ignore the neighborhood sinners, build a higher fence, and hope they'll go away.

But what example did Jesus set? Nothing is clearer in the Gospels than this: Jesus befriended sinners and rebuked the self-righteous.

THE RIGHTEOUSNESS OF THE PHARISEES

Establishing Their Own Righteousness

What do you know about the Pharisees? Your opinion of them is probably negative. But think about this—

45

- They believed in God as Creator and Ruler of the universe.
- They acknowledged that humans are guilty of sin and responsible to God.
- They anticipated eternity, the resurrection, and a coming judgment.
- They looked for a Messiah to come to deliver His people.
- They believed that the Law and the Prophets were given by God.
- They read, studied, obeyed, and preserved the Scriptures.
- They prayed.
- They strove for moral purity.

You probably do these things too! But the Pharisees went much further. Not only did they work diligently to keep every "jot and tittle" of the laws that fill whole books of the Old Testament but they also created new ones. Thousands of extrabiblical dietary, sanitary, and social-conduct regulations—the "oral law"—controlled their lives. It's tedious even to read them, and not even their most diligent, devoted students mastered their full requirements. But they certainly tried!

1. Paul was trained as a Pharisee. What did he say about himself and the "traditions of [his] fathers" (Galatians 1:14; Philippians 3:4–6)?

_____

_____

Theirs might have been a harmless though futile quest, except for this fact: the Pharisees relied on their keeping of religious rules as proof of their spirituality, regardless of the condition of their hearts. Their focus was on outward, not inner, righteousness. As long as they acted right, they believed, they were in a right standing before God.

2. What did Paul, after his conversion, think about such self-righteous Jews (Romans 10:2–3)?

_____

What did they have that's desirable but defective?

_____

What are the two kinds of righteousness?

_____

Which one had they not surrendered to?

_____

What were they trying to create on their own?

_____

3. What two kinds of righteousness does Paul contrast in Philippians 3:9?

_____

How sad to work so hard at the impossible task of making yourself acceptable to God through your own goodness when the gospel offers salvation freely—"by grace through faith." Salvation is "not of yourselves; it is the gift of God, not of works, lest any man should boast" (Ephesians 2:8–9).

4. Nevertheless, many still follow the rules of their own religion in hopes of earning salvation. What are some religious practices people today trust in to merit heaven?

_____

_____

That kind of wrong thinking is prevalent everywhere, not only in cults and false religions but even among regular churchgoers. While one of our friends was planting a church in a small Southern town, he interviewed folks on the street, asking them how they knew they were going to heaven. Even in that gospel-saturated, Bible-Belt community, their answers echoed the spirit of the Pharisees:

47

- "I've been going to church since before I was born."
- "I believe in God, and I'm doing the best I can."
- "I keep the Ten Commandments—or at least I'm trying."
- "I pray every single day."
- "I was baptized when I was twelve."
- "I've been catechized and confirmed."
- "I've been a tither for forty years."
- "I'm trying to be good enough for God to let me in."

How would you answer that question? My husband, Dave, was taught to tithe by his dad when he was only seven years old. He gave even more than a tenth (a nickel from his allowance of thirty-five cents!) Did his tithing make him righteous before God? He was also baptized before he was saved. Did the baptismal water wash away any of his sins? After Dave accepted Christ as Savior at age twenty, he continued giving out of love for the Lord, not as a way of obtaining salvation, and he was scripturally baptized.

Judging Jesus' Righteousness

It would be funny if it weren't so sad—the Pharisees judged Jesus' righteousness defective simply because He did not keep their manmade laws! After He had on the Sabbath healed a man born blind, some of them declared, "This man is not of God, because he keepeth not the sabbath day." When others asked the troubling question "How can a man that is a sinner do such miracles?" the formerly blind man pointed out the obvious, "If this man were not of God, he could do nothing" (John 9:16, 33). But the Pharisees disregarded the obvious and rejected the Messiah.

5. What did they criticize about Him and His disciples in Mark 7:1–5?

_____

_____

This wasn't ordinary washing of hands and dishes but was an elaborate, carefully prescribed cleansing ritual.

6. What did Jesus say to reprimand them in verses 6–9?

_____

_____

The Pharisees believed that people could be made unclean before God by what touched them from the outside. That's why they avoided contact with what their laws declared to be unclean foods, objects, or people (such as Gentiles) and why their rinsing rituals were so important. Jesus, however, taught a completely different doctrine to the gathered crowd in verses 14–16.

7. What did He teach in these verses?

_____

8. This was such a new idea that the disciples asked their Master to explain it to them (verses 17–23). What sins did He say come "from within, out of the heart of men"?

_____

_____

_____

_____

_____

9. What else did the Pharisees find objectionable in Matthew 12:1–13?

_____

"Have you not read?" The Pharisees were probably irritated by His knowledge and accurate application of their Scriptures, and it's clear that they became infuriated by what He said in verses 6–8. Who did Jesus claim to be?

_____

How did the Pharisees respond to His claim (verse 14)?

_____

THE HYPOCRISY OF THE PHARISEES

Trying to present an aura of righteous perfection will always lead to hypocrisy, for in the flesh there is "no good thing" (Romans 7:18). We are all sinners, flawed and incapable of obtaining perfection and righteousness even by our most disciplined efforts.

> But we are all as an unclean thing, and all our righteousnesses are as filthy rags; and we all do fade as a leaf; and our iniquities, like the wind, have taken us away. (Isaiah 64:6)

> For the flesh lusteth against the Spirit, and the Spirit against the flesh: and these are contrary the one to the other: so that ye cannot do the things that ye would. (Galatians 5:17)

At the beginning of His ministry, Jesus publicly charged the Pharisees with hypocrisy while preaching the Sermon on the Mount at the beginning of His ministry. In one of His final public messages, He pronounced on them a series of woes. And in between, He engaged them in lively debate.

THE SERMON ON THE MOUNT

10. Read Matthew 5:17–20. Where can you find "the Law and the Prophets"? (Hint: you probably have them close at hand right now!)

_____

11. Why did Jesus come to earth (Matthew 5:17–18; Romans 10:4)?

_____

12. When did He fulfill all the requirements of the law, setting us free from its bondage (Ephesians 2:14–16)?

_____

No one can be saved by keeping the law. Instead of making us righteous, God's law only helps us discover how sinful we are. As we try and fail, try and fail, try and fail, we come to see that personal perfection is impossible. Why then, in Matthew 5:20, does Jesus seem to call for perfection as the means of entering heaven?

13. What is the only way for you to possess righteousness that "exceeds the righteousness of the scribes and Pharisees" (Romans 4:3–8)?

The Pharisees wanted righteousness, and that's good. The problem was that they were trying to achieve it on their own. In Matthew 5, Jesus moves from topic to topic (murder, adultery, divorce, oaths, retaliation, love), contradicting the teachings of the Pharisees. "You have heard . . . ," Jesus said over and over, "But I say to you . . . ," pointing out the contrast between their insistence on outward actions and His on inward attitudes.

In Matthew 6, He showed His disciples several specific ways to be different from the Pharisees.

Giving

14. What kind of show did they put on as they "gave alms [charitable giving]" (Matthew 6:1–4)?

Prayer

15. Where and how did they pray (verses 5–15)? Why?

Where are you to pray? To whom?

Do you have a prayer closet of your own? It may not be an actual closet (mine's a recliner!), but finding a quiet place for regular, private talks with God will enhance your prayer life. Whenever you go there, your heart will warm and your thoughts will turn toward Him. Set aside a prayer closet today—any spot away from distractions, where you and your Lord can meet.

What is not supposed to be part of your prayers (verse 7)? Why (verse 8)?

What else is essential for your prayers to be heard and answered (verses 14–15)?

Fasting

16. What did the Pharisees do to gain attention and praise for their fasting (verses 16–18)?

Instead, how are you to practice this discipline?

Jesus' teaching is obvious: just performing religious deeds, even with a sincere heart, cannot produce righteousness. Only a righteousness that "exceeds the righteousness of the scribes and Pharisees" will satisfy God's demands. But when you are made "perfect in Christ Jesus" (Colossians 1:28), His perfection is imputed to you—put on your account as though it is your own! How glorious that is! What freedom it gives!

17. Jesus never let up on the self-righteous Pharisees. What

did He call them in Matthew 12:38–39?

_____

What did he call them in Matthew 16:1–3?

_____

18. What did He call their doctrine in Matthew 16:5–12?

_____

What is the danger of even a little bit of self-righteousness?

_____

Near the end of His time with them, Jesus once more discussed the Pharisees with His disciples.

19. Read Matthew 23:1–12 and list their behaviors and attitudes the disciples were not to imitate.

_____

_____

_____

_____

_____

20. In verses 13–36, Jesus detailed for the Pharisees why they faced judgment. He was blunt—even harsh—as He pronounced woes upon them. He dealt this severely only with one group of people. What did He call them?

Verses 13, 14, 15, 23, 25, 27, 29

_____

Verses 16, 24

_____

Verses 17, 19

_____

Verse 33

_____

Jesus also used some memorable metaphors, making comparisons that would be especially meaningful to the Pharisees. According to the Old Testament law, insects and elephants were unclean animals, not to be eaten. To avoid accidentally swallowing an insect, Pharisees would drink from cups covered with a filtering cloth.

21. According to verse 24, what did they swallow?

_____

What was Jesus saying about them?

_____

22. Because they were zealous about ritual cleanliness, the Pharisees were obsessed with the minutiae of washing dishes. What did Jesus compare them to in verse 25?

_____

What did He tell them to do in verse 26?

_____

23. They also believed that to touch the dead or step on a grave would make them ceremonially unclean. What did Jesus compare them to in verses 27–28?

_____

It's no wonder that the Pharisees hated Him, and that they conspired to send Him to the cross. But when He died there, He was dying for their sins—the very sins He had exposed and denounced. Though Jesus hated the Pharisees' self-righteousness, He loved them enough to die for them.

THE HOPE OF THE PHARISEES

Some Pharisees did believe on Him! The Pharisee Nicodemus first came to talk to Jesus after dark so that no one would see him. John 3:1–21 records their extraordinary conversation about the new birth—a classic and beloved passage of Scripture. It was to this sincerely seeking Pharisee that Jesus spoke these sweet words: "For God so loved the world, that he gave his only begotten Son, that whosoever believeth in him should not perish, but have everlasting life" (3:16). Isn't it wonderful to think of Jesus first speaking this promise of instant, unconditional forgiveness to a Pharisee? Everyone, no matter how self-righteous or sinful, is offered the same gift of salvation.

24. Did Nicodemus believe? When he defended Jesus before other Pharisees and Jewish rulers in John 7:45–52, he may have already become a secret believer. How did he finally publicly declare his love for Christ (John 19:38–40)?

As far as I can discover, the sect of the Pharisees doesn't exist today. I've never seen anyone blow a trumpet to announce his offering or shout a loud prayer in the middle of the mall. But the Pharisees' spirit is still around. Right now God is looking at your heart. What does He see? Are you trusting in your own righteousness to save you from sin, or can you say with Isaiah, "I will greatly rejoice in the Lord, my soul shall be joyful in my God; for he hath clothed me with the garments of salvation, he hath covered me with the robe of righteousness" (Isaiah 61:10).

If there be one stitch in the celestial garment of our righteousness which we are to insert ourselves, then we are lost; but this is our confidence, the Lord who began will perfect. He has done it all, must do it all, and will do it all.

–Charles H. Spurgeon

Maybe you have realized during this lesson that, like the Pharisees, you have trusted your own outward goodness, not the perfect righteousness of Jesus, for salvation. You can ask Him right now to save you by praying a prayer like this:

Dear God,
I know that I am a sinner; I deserve only eternal death, separated from you in hell, as punishment for my sin. I understand that I cannot save myself by my own efforts. Right now I turn away from my sin and all my efforts to redeem myself. I now trust Jesus Christ alone as my Savior from sin and make Him my Lord. Please cleanse my heart and make me a new creation. I give you my life. Help me to live for You. Amen.

Jesus! What a friend for sinners!
Jesus! Lover of my soul.
Friends may fail me, foes assail me,
He, my Savior, makes me whole.

—*J. Wilbur Chapman*

Jesus is the friend of sinners! Those words comfort and encourage us. But when the Pharisees and scribes "murmured, saying, This man receiveth sinners, and eateth with them" (Luke 15:2), it was no compliment. Those Jewish leaders, so fastidious about keeping their religious rules, showed little compassion for anyone less pious than themselves. They considered it a disgrace to eat, drink, or have social contact with publicans or immoral persons. But Jesus did not avoid or condemn social outcasts. He actively sought them out! He treated all lost souls with kindness and mercy, for they were the ones He had come "to seek and to save" (Luke 19:10).

Jesus' association with outcasts set Him apart from religious leaders who were more concerned with their reputation than with the needy around them. It also identified Him as the Messiah.

1. Read Luke 4:16–30. Where was Jesus teaching?

_____

2. What five specific things would the Messiah do, according to verse 18?

_____

_____

3. What prophet was Jesus quoting? (The passage is in chapter 61, verses 1–2 of that book.)

---

4. After Jesus read this passage detailing the coming ministry of the Messiah, He rolled up the scroll, gave it back to be returned to its case, and sat down. As everyone in the synagogue stared at Him, what did He say (verse 21)?

Unmistakably, Jesus was claiming to be the Messiah. The people of His hometown did not believe Him, as verses 28–30 make very clear! But soon His works proved His claim true. While John the Baptist was in prison, he sent two of his disciples to ask Jesus if He was the Messiah: "Art thou he that should come? or look we for another?" Read the account of that conversation in Luke 7:19–23.

5. Jesus did not directly answer their questions, but what did they see happen "in that same hour" (verse 21)?

What proof of His messiahship did Jesus ask John's disciples to relate to their master (verse 22)?

John the Baptist, hearing the report of his disciples, understood that Jesus was doing miracles that only the Messiah could do. We don't usually consider the gospel being preached to the poor to be a miracle, but to outcasts, so used to being rejected, it must have seemed the greatest miracle of all when they were invited to receive God's mercy and grace. Zacchaeus was one of those social outcasts. He was shunned and scorned because of his occupation. Luke, the only Gospel writer to tell his story, prepares us for it in Luke 18.

6. What is the point of the story Jesus told in verses 9–14?

_____

7. Why did the wealthy young leader decide that he would not follow Jesus (verses 18–23)?

_____

8. For whom did Jesus do a miracle in verses 35–43?

_____

By the time He entered Jericho (on the way to Jerusalem to be crucified), Jesus had already made several things clear: righteousness comes by way of humble repentance, not through self-glorifying religious acts; sacrificial obedience proves saving faith; and salvation is offered to all who acknowledge their need and come to Him, regardless of social status. Now He was about to give a dramatic object lesson of those truths to all who were watching.

"And Jesus entered and passed through Jericho" (Luke 19:1). This was a prosperous city known for impressive architecture and beautiful palms, a place for travelers to rest before the tiring and dangerous climb to Jerusalem. As a crossroads for merchant traffic, Jericho was home to many collectors of import/export customs, tolls, and taxes on merchandise. Zacchaeus was one of them.

9. What important details about Zacchaeus do we learn in Luke 19:2–3, 9?

His occupation

_____

His wealth

_____

His physical stature

_____

His religion

The heavy tax assessments collected by men such as Zacchaeus were paid into the treasuries of the Roman Empire. No one really enjoys paying taxes, but the Judeans especially hated them as symbols of the oppressive rule of that tyrannical government. It's easy to see why. There was no standard code, so tax rates were indefinite. Because some tax funds were used to finance the worship of false gods, some Jews regarded paying them as sacrilegious.

10. What did Jesus say about paying taxes (Matthew 22:21)?

As obedient subjects of the human powers established by God, believers are to give, as a matter of conscience, "tribute to whom tribute is due; custom to whom custom" (Romans 13:1–7)—even when we'd rather not!

What especially infuriated the Jews was that some of their own countrymen had contracted with Rome to collect the hated taxes. These men—called publicans—gathered as much as they could get away with. They gave the government what it demanded and kept the rest for themselves. With the fearful power of Rome behind them, they practiced taxation tyranny and became exceedingly rich. They also were despised as cheats, extortioners, and betrayers of their fellow Jews. Because they were almost universally dishonest (think mafia, not the IRS), the word *publican* came to mean a person without moral principles. Jesus understood this and used publicans as illustrations as He taught.

11. What did He say about them in Matthew 5:43–47?

---

12. When a Christian brother who has sinned and been reproved refuses to repent, how did Jesus say to treat him (Matthew 18:15–17)?

What does that reveal about how people treated publicans?

_____

13. Who were publicans classified with in the following verses?

Matthew 9:10–11

_____

Matthew 18:17

_____

Matthew 21:31

_____

Zacchaeus was not just an ordinary tax collector. He was the "chief of the publicans." His townspeople must have cringed whenever they said his name, for it comes from a Hebrew word meaning "pure." They believed (with good reason) that he was filthy instead! They shunned Zacchaeus and certainly expected Jesus to avoid his company too. But Jesus surprised them all. He entered Jericho followed by a crowd of believers and curiosity-seekers. With about fifteen more miles to travel to Jerusalem, along a road notorious for robbers, Jesus needed a place to eat and spend the night before the journey. Read Luke 19:1–9 as though you've never before heard (or sung!) this story.

Zacchaeus may have been sitting at his tax collection table or near his office window when he heard the clamor of the crowd as Jesus passed by. He knew he would not be welcome among the townspeople who hated him, but he risked their insults and ran out into the streets anyway. Too short to see over the crowd, he climbed up into a sycamore tree, into sturdy boughs overhanging the street. When was the last time you climbed a tree? Unless you're a tree-trimmer or fruit-picker, it's likely been a long time! It was an undignified thing for a governmental official like Zacchaeus to do. What do you think could have made him so unself-conscious, so determined "to see Jesus, who he was"?

All over the world, people want to know Who Jesus is. Are you telling them? Our daughter Susannah meets them often.

> I was browsing in the bookstore when a student said, "Excuse me, can you tell me what this word means?" As an English teacher in China, I answer that question often. I glanced quickly down at the key chain she was holding, prepared to give a brief definition of whatever word it was that she didn't know. But this word would require much more: J—E—S—U—S.

> I wanted to say, "What does this word mean? Well, this word means the difference between life and death. It means salvation from everything that is wrong in the world. It can mean eternal joy for you." Instead, after a moment to steady my voice, I just said, "Jesus. Jesus. The Son of God."

> "Oh, yes," she said. "Thank you."

Maybe Zacchaeus had discovered, as so many have, that wealth cannot satisfy. Riches are deceitful (Mark 4:19), for they promise peace and joy but deliver neither. Money makes its owners rich in material goods but destitute of true riches. And Zacchaeus craved something more. Maybe he had heard of the remarkable change in life of Matthew. Read Matthew's own description of his encounter with Christ in Matthew 9:9. Matthew (also called by his Jewish name "Levi") was an official sitting "at the receipt of custom"—in the tax office, or custom house. The men who worked in that setting were considered to be the worst among the publicans—worthless and hopeless, excluded from any religious activities with other Jews.

14. Matthew may have overheard Jesus' words and seen His deeds, for he sat and worked near where Jesus taught the crowds who gathered along the seaside. Which miracles had Matthew probably heard the locals discussing (Matthew 8:23–9:8)?

_____

_____

Through His work, Matthew would have known the Galilean fishermen who had already become Jesus' committed disciples. His heart must have been prepared and yearning for salvation because when the Savior came by, He said only two words to Matthew: "Follow me."

15. What did Matthew do (Luke 5:28)?

_____

What does this interchange reveal about Jesus?

_____

About Matthew?

_____

If you had been nearby when Jesus said, "Follow Me," you would have been shocked to see Matthew stand up and follow after Jesus. He would have seemed the least likely in the crowd to become a disciple. But Jesus knew he was ready. We cannot see into hearts, as Jesus does. We do not know where God has been working, softening and convicting sinners and drawing them to Himself. But He is always at work, even when we cannot see it, even in the hearts of the most unlikely people, rich or poor, prominent or outcast.

16 Who among your acquaintances seems the least likely to follow Christ?

_____

How should this story of Jesus and Matthew affect the way you look at them?

_____

63

How should it affect your witnessing?

17. What did Matthew do next (Luke 5:29)?

Luke calls this a "mega-feast" with a great multitude of guests. Who came?

18. Why do you think Matthew held this feast?

19. How did the Pharisees and scribes react (Luke 5:30)?

The Pharisees and the teachers of the law found Jesus' conduct most objectionable and challenged the disciples to explain why Jesus would fellowship with tax collectors and sinners. The inference was that if Jesus were what He claimed to be, He would have sought their company rather than the company of those with whom He was then eating.[1]

20. The disciples didn't answer their challenge, but Jesus did. What did He say (Luke 5:31–32)?

Who were "they who are whole" (or thought they were)?

Who were "they that are sick" (and knew they were)?

Those who believed themselves well were actually sick with sin; those who recognized their own sinful condition were eager to be made well.

It's not hard to imagine the questions in Zacchaeus's mind when he saw that Jesus mingled with publicans: "Every other Jew hates us. Why is this man Jesus different? Why does He associate with us? How does He change people? Can He change me?" Zacchaeus had chosen to be a publican and to indulge in the wrongdoing that went along with his occupation. But now he longed to be made clean.

Just as He did with Matthew, Jesus passed by, saw a publican sitting (this time up in a tree), and spoke to him. He knew exactly who Zacchaeus was, why he was there, and what he needed. "Zacchaeus," He said. "Make haste, and come down; for today I must abide at thy house." Here Jesus did what He did nowhere else in Scripture—invited Himself to someone else's home. That's the sort of the thing you do only with a very close friend. Jesus saw Zacchaeus not as he was but as he soon would be.

The Pharisees reacted as usual, grumbling and complaining that Jesus had "gone to be guest with a man that is a sinner" (Luke 19:7). Their complaints, though, were actually high praise!

> This Man, who towers above all other men, holy, harmless, undefiled, and separate from sinners—this Man receiveth sinners. This Man, who is no other than the eternal God, before whom angels veil their faces—this Man receiveth sinners. That any of us should be willing to seek after the lost is nothing wonderful—they are of our own race; but that He, the offended God, against whom the transgression has been committed, should take upon Himself the form of a servant, and bear the sin of many, and should then be willing to receive the vilest of the vile, this is marvelous.

> When Jesus receives sinners, He has not some out-of-doors reception place . . . where He charitably entertains them as men do passing beggars, but He opens the golden gates of His royal heart, and receives the sinner right into Himself— yea, He admits the humble penitent into personal union and

makes Him a member of His body, of His flesh, and of His bones. There was never such a receiving as His!

—Charles H. Spurgeon

Zacchaeus was a social outcast because of his occupation. He was accepted by Christ not because he changed jobs but because he put his faith in Jesus Christ as Savior. I wish I could have watched as Zacchaeus "made haste, and came down, and received him joyfully." I would have enjoyed seeing these two moving through the grumbling crowd to Zacchaeus's house, where the sinner opened both his home and his heart to the Savior. I would have loved to have overheard their dinner conversation! We know no details of that evening but this one: at its end, Zacchaeus was transformed.

21. What evidence do we have that his salvation had thoroughly, instantly changed him (Luke 19:8)?

Zacchaeus was not saved by his good deeds, but his actions showed that he was a new creature. He showed his faith by his works (James 2:18)—going far beyond what the Jewish law required for repaying money gained by fraud (Leviticus 6:1–5). No wonder Jesus exclaimed in Luke 19:9, "This day is salvation come to this house." The lost had been sought and saved! Despite huge hindrances—wealth, a despised occupation, and social exile—Zacchaeus, a son of Abraham, had found a Savior and a new life as a true son of God! If you, too, know Jesus Christ as Lord and Savior, follow the example of the One Who went out of His way to seek the outcast. The incarnate Jesus was a true friend of sinners, and we should we be just like Him.

Jesus spoke His good news to people in the streets, on the hillsides, and along the shores of Lake Galilee. They saw Him heal the sick, cast out demons, multiply the loaves and fishes, even resurrect the dead. Some who heard His words and saw His miracles believed and followed Him. Others rejected Him. Many weren't sure what to think. Those folks must have wondered, "If that man isn't the Christ, who is he, and how does he do those tricks?"

On Sabbath days, Jesus often taught in synagogues. That's where Simon the Pharisee met Him and invited Him to his home for dinner. Perhaps he wanted to observe Jesus up close and question Him informally. Was Simon looking for a reason to believe or for an excuse to reject? Or was he just being polite? We don't know what his motives were, but when an outcast showed up uninvited, the meal turned into a point of spiritual decision. Before dinner was over, Simon had made up his mind about Jesus Christ. Read the story in Luke 7:36–50.

BACKGROUND

Understanding some of the social customs of Bible times will help you set the scene. When a guest arrived in a home for a meal, the host would greet him with a kiss of friendship. A slave would remove the guest's sandals, pour water over his dusty feet, rub them with his hands, and dry them with a towel. Then the servant would anoint the guest's head with cooling, scented oil.

1. Was Jesus welcomed with these ordinary acts of courtesy (Luke 7:44-46)?

2. Why do you think Simon neglected his duties as a host?

In New Testament times, guests in a noble home would often be entertained in a *triclinium*, a formal dining room with three tables arranged at right angles around a low, square serving table. Diners would recline on couches set beside the tables, leaning on their left arms and eating with their right hands, their bare feet extending behind them. The door to a house where a guest was being entertained would often be left open so that spectators could wander in to watch and listen—but not to eat. That is how an uninvited woman slipped inside Simon's home.

The Cast

Only two people spoke during this drama: Simon and Jesus. Nothing the other people present (Jesus' disciples, invited Pharisees and other guests, family members, and servants) said or did is recorded. But the actions of that one woman made an impact on all who were present. Simon's reaction to her revealed his judging, condemning heart. Jesus' reaction, in contrast, showed His loving, accepting spirit.

We don't know this woman's name. Some have mistakenly taught that she was Mary, the sister of Martha and Lazarus. Mary did anoint Jesus' feet in a similar way (Matthew 26:6–13; Mark 14:3–9; John 12:2–8), but this is a different person, as you can see when you compare the two accounts.

The Location
Luke 7—somewhere in Galilee
Mary—in Bethany, near Jerusalem
The Time
Luke 7—at the beginning of Jesus' earthly ministry
Mary—six days before His crucifixion
The Homeowner
Luke 7—Simon the Pharisee
Mary—Simon the leper

The Woman

Luke 7—a public sinner

Mary—one of Jesus' close, devoted friends

Others have guessed that the woman was Mary Magdalene. But Luke introduces her at the beginning of the next chapter as a new character, one "out of whom went seven devils" (Luke 8:2). We also have no reason to believe that Mary Magdalene was a public sinner—only that she had once been demon-possessed.

ACT ONE

The curtain rises, and the action starts: "He went into the Pharisee's house, and sat down to meat" (Luke 7:36). Jesus accepted social invitations, mingling with people so that He could talk to them about the kingdom of heaven. He attended a wedding at Cana (John 2:1–2), took part in a feast at Matthew's home (Luke 5:29), and ate in the home of his Bethany friends (Luke 10:38–39).

"And, behold, a woman in the city, which was a sinner, when she knew that Jesus sat at meat in the Pharisee's house" entered the room (7:37). All she had to do to shock the diners and other onlookers was to walk into the house. We aren't told her specific sin, but the phrase "which was a sinner" tells us that she was known as a person of bad character. Her appearance, especially with her long hair worn loosely, would, in those days, have identified her as a harlot. Speaking to someone like her was taboo for the Pharisees. Touching her would make them ceremonially unclean, so they would cross the street to avoid an accidental encounter. To share food and drink with such a woman was unthinkable.

3. If you were directing this scene on a stage, how would you tell the characters to react? What looks would be on their faces? What would they be whispering to each other?

_____

_____

_____

I once watched a young woman walk into church with a friend who had been praying for her salvation. The visitor was inappropriately dressed for a Sunday morning service—at least in the opinion of a lady sitting near me, who mumbled out loud to nobody in particular, "What's wrong with her, coming to church looking like that? Doesn't she know how to dress right?"

4. What do you think about that reaction?

Have you ever driven through a city district where public sinners—drug dealers and users, drunks and prostitutes, homeless folks and beggars—were sprawled on the sidewalks or clustered on the corners? What was your reaction?

Most of us who are normally insulated from such sights feel a mingling of curiosity and revulsion, seeing them as a personal danger and public nuisance. We lock our car doors and speed back to our safe and comfortable enclaves, putting those people out of mind as quickly as we put them out of sight. That day in Simon's home everyone else was stunned and dismayed by the arrival of the sinful woman—but not Jesus. He had been expecting her. She must have known how the others would react, but at that moment, to that woman, Jesus was the only One Whose opinion mattered. That gave her the courage to come.

5. What did she bring with her to Simon's house (verse 37)?

Alabaster is a translucent white, gray, or yellow gypsum stone with a lovely, fine texture. A box like this, filled with expensive perfumed ointment, would have been one of her most precious possessions. Maybe she had planned to hand it to Jesus as a gift.

6. Rather than just offering the box, what did she do with it (verse 38)?

_____

Perhaps when she approached Jesus, she noticed that He had been slighted by His host. She began kissing His dusty feet and bathing them with her streaming tears. Then she anointed them with her perfume and wiped them dry with her hair. Sweet fragrance from the alabaster box filled the room and her sobbing filled the silence. The hush was also filled with unspoken questions ("What's wrong with her?") and unvoiced hostility. What the shocked Pharisees and guests did not understand was that she was there not as an intruder but as a disciple of Jesus Christ. She was offering Him not just a gift but her whole self. "I believe!" she was saying. "I am Yours! I will follow You!" As she adored and worshiped her Lord, she noticed no one but Him.

Jesus asked her no questions, for since He was God, He already knew her and why she had come. It's likely that He had seen her earlier—maybe on a hillside, watching with longing from the edge of the crowd, listening carefully as He offered forgiveness and cleansing. He had seen the hope rise in her eyes as she began to understand: "He can help me! He can change me!" And she had accepted the salvation Jesus offered. Her heart had been washed clean, her sin as fully gone as if it had never been. When she heard that Jesus was at Simon's house, she made it her mission to find Him so that she could thank Him and worship Him.

7. We already know she was brave. What other adjectives would you choose to describe her?

_____

8. Love is demonstrated by giving. Have you ever sacrificed an "alabaster box" to the Lord? What motivated your gift?

_____

If you have never made that kind of sacrifice, why do you think you haven't?

_____

9. In Luke 7:39, Simon, the homeowner and host, finally spoke. Who was he talking to?

_____

10. What conclusion had he come to while watching this scene in his dining room?

_____

11. What was the basis for his reasoning?

_____

Simon, oblivious to the astonishing transformation of the sinful woman, had put the worst possible interpretation on this touching scene. He was aghast that Jesus would allow an outcast to touch Him, for that was a major violation of the Pharisees' rules. Judging Jesus Christ by manmade religious regulations, Simon concluded that He was not a true prophet. At that moment, Simon rejected Jesus Christ—and the curtain falls on act one.

ACT TWO

12. As the next scene opens, Jesus spoke, "answering" Simon (verse 40). What was He answering?

_____

13. According to Matthew 9:4 and 12:25, how was Jesus able to answer Simon?

_____

Then Jesus (as He often did while teaching) told a story

followed by a question. The story was a parable—a short, simple tale that illustrates truth. Read it in Luke 7:41–42.

14. Who are the three characters?

_____

_____

What did each debtor owe?

_____

_____

How did the creditor respond?

_____

_____

_____

15. What question did Jesus then ask?

_____

Simon probably squirmed as he responded, for the moral of the story was painfully obvious. Jesus praised him for giving the right answer: "Thou hast rightly judged" (verse 43). But the truth is, of course, that Simon had already wrongly judged both the woman and Jesus Himself. Now he had unwillingly rebuked himself.

16. What was the lesson of Jesus' parable?

_____

17. Jesus tenderly chided Simon and praised the outcast. What were the differences between them (verses 44–46)?

_____

18. What made them act in such different ways (verse 47)?

19. Jesus spoke kindly in order not to embarrass His host, but the gentle reproach in His words was unmistakable. In contrast, He made two thrilling announcements to the woman. What were they?

Verse 48—

Verse 50—

Simon had thought that Jesus didn't recognize the sinner in the room. But He did, of course. It just wasn't the one Simon thought it was! Consider the contrasts between Simon and the woman.

- Simon's sins were invisible. Hers were public.
- Simon stood proudly upright. She bowed humbly.
- Simon was unrepentant. She was contrite.
- Simon rejected. She believed.

What happened next? Did Simon ever believe on Jesus? Did the woman live happily ever after? I'm looking forward to meeting her in heaven so I can find out!

If you were auditioning for this drama and were told that there were two parts open for casting—a respected religious leader and a sinful outcast—which role would you have wanted? But now, knowing the end of the story, which would you rather be? There's irony here, for the sinner is praised as a saint, and the "saint" is exposed as the real sinner. For just a few minutes as we read Luke 7 we are allowed to see people the way God sees them.

20. How does God see people according to 1 Samuel 16:7?

The outcast loved much because she knew how much she had been forgiven. Simon loved little, not because he had fewer sins to be forgiven but because he thought he didn't need forgiveness. To offer the Lord the love He deserves, you must learn—and never, never, never forget—how much you have been forgiven. If you were saved as an adult, you probably find it easy to recall the years you wasted living for yourself, rebelling against God, disregarding His love, and rejecting His grace. Don't wallow in regret, for Jesus Christ forgives completely and changes people from the inside out. But do remember the past. If you forget what He has saved you from and where your sin could have led you, you will lose your passion. You will begin to act more like Simon and less like the forgiven woman.

My cousin and his wife are in their first term of missionary service in Africa—a bit unusual for a couple their age—and nothing less than a miracle for those of us who have known and loved him during his difficult past. He writes,

> God has made some wonderful changes in me. Ten years ago I would have laughed if someone asked me to become a missionary. However, the Lord God planted gospel seeds in me at a young age. They started growing, sunk their roots deep into my spirit, and are now blooming. I can't believe it. Me—a drunk, drugged-out hippie, adulterous lying thief, now changed by the blood of Jesus Christ into a man of God. Hallelujah! Glory to God! Only He could make such a change! He picked me up out of the miry clay, placed my feet on the Rock, cleansed me with His blood, and I have pledged fealty to Him until we meet face to face.

Because my cousin cannot forget all he has been forgiven, he fervently loves and serves his Savior. But maybe, like me, you were saved when you were little, before you had an opportunity to give in to many of the world's temptations. Both before and after your salvation, you were a good little girl (mostly). Surely, you may think, He didn't have that much to forgive me for! But the truth is this: even as children, you and I were sinful rebels against God.

21. Find answers to the following questions in Exodus 20:1–17.

Whenever you wanted what another child had, what were you guilty of?

_____

When you stuck coins or candy into your pocket that weren't yours, what were you doing?

_____

When you disobeyed or pretended not to hear your parents' instructions, which commandment were you breaking?

_____

When you blamed your own wrong on someone else, which of God's rules were you disobeying?

_____

Every time you put yourself first and insisted on your own way, which commandment were you violating?

_____

Foolishness was bound in our hearts even as children (Proverbs 22:15), and except for our parents' training and discipline, we would still be horrid! Our heart is still "deceitful above all things, and desperately wicked: who can know it?" (Jeremiah 17:9). When I was a teenager, our Sunday school teacher asked the girls in our class to remember our most recent sin. (It didn't take long!) Then she said, "That one sin would be enough to send you to hell and Christ to the cross to die for you." She was right. When I add to that one sin all I have committed since, I'm overwhelmed at all I have been forgiven.

Every sin is a serious offense to God. Read Galatians 5:19. (Look up the meanings of any obscure words.) Do the same with

Ephesians 4:25–31; 5:3–4; Colossians 3:8–9; and Titus 3:2–3. Notice how many of these are unseen sins of the mind and spirit like Simon's, known only to God and yourself.

22. Read 1 Peter 2:1. List the five sins named. Which of these sins do you tolerate or indulge?

_____

_____

_____

If you will answer this honestly, you will be humbled by your capacity for sin.

> If I will take an honest look at myself, becoming fully aware of my so-called innocence and putting it to the test, I am very likely to have a rude awakening that what Jesus Christ said is true, and I will be appalled at the possibilities of the evil and the wrong within me. . . . If I have never been an openly rude and abusive person, the only reason is my own cowardice coupled with the sense of protection I receive from living a civilized life. But when I am open and completely exposed before God, I find that Jesus Christ is right in His diagnosis of me. The only thing that truly provides protection is the redemption of Jesus Christ. If I will simply hand myself over to Him, I will never have to experience the terrible possibilities that lie within my heart.
>
> *—Oswald Chambers*

Every sinner, *good or bad*, public or private, deserves to be an outcast from God forever and can do nothing to save her own soul. But on the cross, Jesus Christ offered Himself as an atoning sacrifice "for the sins of the whole world' (1 John 2:2). None of us has any hope apart from His blood—but through it, He offers full, free, forever forgiveness!

> And when they had nothing to pay, he frankly forgave them both. (Luke 7:42)

The blood of Jesus Christ his Son cleanseth us
from all sin. (1 John 1:7)

How much Jesus loved outcasts like Zacchaeus and the "woman who was a sinner." How much He loves you and me! How we ought to love Him in return! And surely, as we recall all we have been forgiven, we will be moved to imitate His spirit toward those that others shun.

LESSON 8

When this story takes place, Jesus' years on earth were coming to an end. As opposition from angry, unbelieving Jews escalated, He withdrew to a private place "beyond the Jordan" (John 10:40). Soon He would travel to Jerusalem to be tried and crucified. He and His disciples were not far from Bethany when His friends, who lived there, the sisters Mary and Martha, called for help.

THE FAMILY

You are probably familiar with this family because of a famous scene in their home when Mary sat at Jesus' feet while Martha rushed about serving and fretting. All we know about Lazarus is that he was Jesus' friend; that he lived, died, and was buried; and that He was released from his tomb in an astounding demonstration of Jesus' power over death.

1. Read John 11:1–44 carefully. The story opens with the arrival of what simple but poignant message?

_____

We don't know what was wrong with Lazarus, but his illness was both sudden and serious enough for his sisters to send an urgent message to Jesus. Is it different from the kind of message you would have sent? What does its simplicity tell you about their relationship with Jesus?

Somehow the sisters must have known where He was, for they knew where to send their message. Since He was nearby, they must have been sure He would rush to help their brother. There was no need to beg or plead with their Friend, for His affection was unmistakable. Of course, God the Son already knew that Lazarus would become sick and die.

2. In light of that knowledge, what statement in verse 4 seems strange?

_____

3. We know that Jesus—because He was God—could not lie (Titus 1:5) or tell even a half-truth. Why do you think He said this?

_____

In what way was this sickness "not unto death"?

_____

The sickness was "for the glory of God, that the Son of God might be glorified thereby" (John 11:4). That is, of course, one of the purposes for every trial.

> Let this reconcile us to the darkest dispensations of Providence, they are all for the glory of God. This sickness, this loss, or this disappointment, is so; and, if God be glorified, we ought to be satisfied.
>
> –*Matthew Henry*

THE WAITING

4 Read John 11:5–6. Where is the irony in these verses?

_____

_____

_____

Though He knew Lazarus's sisters were waiting anxiously, He didn't hurry. It must have been a terribly hard wait for Mary and Martha. They had sat by Lazarus's bed as his illness worsened. They had heard the rasp of his final breaths and felt searing grief at his death. Now Lazarus wasn't just sick—he was dead. But still

Jesus did not come. Do you think that while they waited, they were tempted to doubt His love? Waiting for God is hard. The psalmists expressed the deep ache that many of us feel while we wait.

> I am weary of my crying: my throat is dried: mine eyes fail while I wait for my God. (Psalm 69:3)

> My soul is also sore vexed: but thou, O Lord, how long? (Psalm 6:3)

> How long wilt thou forget me, O Lord? for ever? How long wilt thou hide thy face from me? (Psalm 13:1)

David once begged God to hurry: "Be pleased, O Lord, to deliver me: O Lord, make haste to help me. . . . Thou art my help and my deliverer; make no tarrying, O my God" (Psalm 40:13, 17); and the prophet Habakkuk asked this agonizing question for many of us, "O Lord, how long shall I cry, and thou wilt not hear?" (Habakkuk 1:2).

Many of the Marys and Marthas of the world, when filled with more pain than faith, have asked: "Can't You see how I am hurting? Why do You make me wait when I need You so much right now?" Have you ever asked those questions? I have. In fact, prayers that seem unheard are my greatest test of faith.

I once prayed consistently and fervently for a need. I did my best to fulfill every scriptural prerequisite for answered prayer. I believed with all my heart that I was praying in His will and that the answer I sought would be for His glory. After many months of persistent prayer, I became angry and impatient. I decided I was wasting my time—nobody was listening!

The problem was not with my eagerness for an answer or with my disappointment at His delay but with the wrong conclusions I reached as I followed my frustration down a twisty trail of doubt. Maybe, I fretted, God's too busy with more important people to listen to me. Maybe my pleas are lost among all the other cries for help. Or maybe He did hear but doesn't love me enough to answer. Annoyed with God for not answering the way I wanted, when I wanted, I stopped praying. I was miserable.

God dealt very gently with His pouting child. One afternoon while I was shopping, He guided my circumstances and provided for me in a way that showed His tender, intimate knowledge of my simplest needs. I broke into tears, right there in the store. I began to pray again for the same familiar request, but with a very different spirit. He still hasn't answered that prayer, and I still talk to Him about it every day. But now I ask serenely, confident that my long-suffering Savior has a very good reason for His delay.

Martha and Mary also must have felt ignored, coping with their grief while Jesus stayed away. Others in the community asked why the One Who had made the blind see hadn't prevented the death of His friend (John 11:37). The truth is, of course, that Jesus' friends are never neglected or unloved—not for one instant. He doesn't delay because He doesn't know, doesn't love, or doesn't care. His delays are for our good. They are designed to accomplish much greater purposes.

Waiting Purifies Motives

5. Read 1 Samuel 1:1–8. What circumstances caused Hannah such agony that she wept and could not eat? At this point, why did she want a child?

_____

_____

Read verses 9–11. Now why did she want a child?

_____

Hannah's prayers began with seeking personal gratification but matured into joyful surrender. As you wait for God to answer, you may find your prayers changing too. First you beg for help. Then you ask for strength to endure. Then you may request grace to accept His will, whatever it is. You may even reach the highest level of prayer: asking God to bring glory to Himself, even at great cost to you, preferring spiritual growth to immediate relief.

Waiting Enhances Joy When the Answer Comes

Have you been aching for something for a very long time? To finally have your longing fulfilled will be "sweet to [your] soul" (Proverbs 13:19)—much more satisfying than if it had been granted quickly!

6. Rewrite Proverbs 13:12 in your own words.

_____

_____

_____

Mary and Martha's brother's healing would have delighted them at any point, but coming as it did after every other resource was exhausted, after hopeful hours by his bed had ended in days of weeping at his tomb, Mary and Martha's joy must have been overwhelming—enough to abbreviate the wait in their memory, and certainly enough to greatly increase their faith when the next crisis came.

> And it shall be said in that day, Lo, this is our God;
> we have waited for him, and he will save us: this is
> the Lord; we have waited for him, we will be glad
> and rejoice in his salvation. (Isaiah 25:9)

Waiting Brings Greater Glory to God

7. How long had Lazarus's body been sealed in his stone crypt (John 11:17, 39)?

_____

Since Lazarus's body had been decaying that long, no one could doubt that he had been thoroughly dead. He had not swooned, fainted, or been in a coma. His resurrection could not be a trick;

it could have no explanation except the miraculous. Because Jesus waited, His deity was confirmed.

8. Whenever the story of the raising of Lazarus is heard and believed, what prophecy comes true (John 11:4)?

_____

Jesus tenderly loved His friends and wanted to relieve their pain, but He desired His Father's glory even more. God's yearning to display His own glory is not a sign of egoism or pride, as it would be in a human. Our desire for glory is a symptom of sinful self-idolatry; it is seeking, like Satan, to receive the glory that is due only to God.

> I will ascend into heaven, I will exalt my throne above the stars of God . . . I will ascend above the heights of the clouds; I will be like the most High." (Isaiah 14:13–14)

Only God, the essence of all perfection, is worthy of glory.

> Who is like unto thee, O Lord, among the gods? who is like thee, glorious in holiness, fearful in praises, doing wonders? (Exodus 15:11)

In eternity, He will receive it in abundance.

> Worthy is the Lamb that was slain to receive power, and riches, and wisdom, and strength, and honour, and glory, and blessing. (Revelation 5:12)

9. List some ways that you can, as you patiently wait for God, bring Him the glory on earth that He deserves but rarely receives.

_____

_____

_____

Waiting Makes Truth Personal

10. Just after His arrival, Martha had a conversation with Jesus about truth (John 11:21–27). What did Martha say she believed?

Verse 21

_____

Verse 22

_____

Verse 24

_____

Verse 27

_____

11. Martha had correct theology. She believed that Jesus was the promised Messiah, with power over life and death. But when Jesus asked for Lazarus's grave to be opened, what was her quick objection (verse 39)?

_____

Martha knew Jesus *could*—but do you think she believed that He *would*? Painful times try theology. We say we know God is love, but do we believe it when life hurts? We know He is good, but do we believe that all He allows is for our good? I once stood in a cemetery looking down at a tiny coffin that held the body of a child I loved. My heart was broken, but even in my sorrow, my faith held firm. I knew—really knew—that I would see that baby again. My faith was tested, and it held. During that crisis, my creed moved from my head to my heart.

Is the Lord dealing with you in the same way? . . . Have you come, like Martha, to a crossroads of overwhelming circumstances where your theology is about to become a very personal belief? This happens only when a personal problem brings the awareness of our personal need. . . . Then, when I stand face to face with Jesus Christ and He says to me, "Do you believe this?" I find that faith is as natural as breathing. And I am staggered when I think how foolish I have been in not trusting Him earlier.

—Oswald Chambers

Waiting Helps Others

12. Even after the delay, Jesus' disciples objected to His traveling back to Judea. Why did they object (John 10:39; 11:8)?

13. What did Thomas expect to happen on this trip (11:16)?

14. They were afraid not only for their Master but for themselves as well, and those fears were based in reality. Read John 11:45–57. What effect did the raising of Lazarus have on Jesus' enemies?

Jesus knew that though the disciples were not going to die with Him right away, they would soon see Him betrayed, tried, and crucified. Dark days were ahead for His loyal but vulnerable friends, and He wanted to prepare them.

15. Read John 11:14–15. What is another reason Jesus delayed His arrival in Bethany?

16. What should the disciples have understood about Jesus after seeing Lazarus raised?

_____

How should it have strengthened them when He was crucified?

_____

The raising of Lazarus after the delay was also an object lesson for the community—another way for Jesus to showcase His deity and add vigor to His disciples' weak faith. All through this chapter, Jesus made belief an issue:

- Verse 26: "Believest thou this?"
- Verse 40: "If thou wouldest believe"
- Verse 42: "That they may believe"

And many who saw the miracle did believe (verse 45). You were not in Bethany that day, but you are also Jesus' follower, and this story can help you. When death frightens you, read John 11 and be assured: your Savior has already conquered death! It has been "swallowed up in victory" (1 Corinthians 15:54). You can say with Job (a model of patient waiting), "For I know that my redeemer liveth, and that he shall stand at the latter day upon the earth; and though after my skin worms destroy this body, yet in my flesh shall I see God" (Job 19:25–26).

JESUS' WEEPING

When Jesus arrived in Bethany, Mary ran to meet Him and fell at His feet weeping. The One she adored, the One Who loved her brother, had come. I understand her tears, because I also run to my compassionate Savior when I am mourning. I understand the tears of "the Jews also weeping which came with her" (John 11:33). Some were Lazarus's sad friends and neighbors. Others may have been professional mourners, hired to wail and beat their breasts. But do you wonder at Jesus' tears? John 11:35 says simply, "Jesus wept." This verse is short on words but long on meaning.

The word used for "weep" does not mean loud wailing, but a spontaneous spurt of tears.

17. When the Jews saw Jesus' tears, what did they think (verse 36)?

_____

If Jesus knew He was about to raise Lazarus from the dead, why would He cry?

_____

Jesus wept because He was totally human as well as totally God. Jesus was "made in the likeness of men . . . found in fashion as a man" (Philippians 2:7–8), and it's human to cry when a friend dies. Since the sinless One wept over Lazarus, we know that tears during bereavement are not sinful. They are an expression of our human nature, and our faith in Christ does not prohibit them.

18. How is the sorrow of a believer different from that of an unbeliever (1 Thessalonians 4:13)?

_____

What is that "hope"?

_____

Jesus cried when His friend died. He will not mock your tears of sorrow. Because of John 11:35, we know He understands. Jesus wept because those He loved were in pain.

19. When you hear that another woman is hurting, what does Romans 12:15 tell you to do?

_____

20. Why is it natural for Christians to empathize with other believers' hurts (1 Corinthians 12:25–27)?

_____

Jesus wept with Mary and Martha even though He knew He was about to relieve their sorrow—just as a loving mother may cry with her child over a throbbing skinned knee though she knows the pain is temporary. The sisters' grief was ended by the clear call of the One with power over death: "Lazarus, come forth!" And he did, "bound hand and foot with graveclothes; and his face . . . bound about with a napkin."

What a sight! I can't imagine their joy! But I wonder—was Lazarus, as he stood there blinking in the sunlight, happy? Had he been to heaven? Had he seen paradise? If so, was he glad to be back on earth? We don't know where Lazarus was between his death and resurrection, but the blessed truth is this: heaven is better than earth. It is nothing to dread! At my mother-in-law's funeral, I suddenly longed to bring her back from heaven for just a few minutes so I could tell her once more how much I had loved and appreciated her. But I knew immediately what she would have said, "Claudia, what in the world did you do that for? Send me back right now!"

Why did Jesus wait when His friends were in pain? He had higher purposes for them than just immediate relief—as He does for you. Why did He weep at His friend's tomb? He wept because He was human and because those He loved were in pain. He will do the same for you.

> Wait on the Lord: be of good courage, and he
> shall strengthen thine heart: wait, I say, on the
> Lord. (Psalm 27:14)

Have you ever had a failure that left you feeling useless? Did you want to hide from God and find it hard to believe that He could ever forgive you? Did you avoid people who knew about your failure, though you knew nothing they could say to shame you could be worse than your own self-accusations? If so, you know how Peter felt when, after repeatedly denying his Lord, he went out and wept bitterly. Studying Peter's story will give you hope, for Jesus dealt tenderly with this disciple who failed.

PETER'S PERSONALITY

The Gospels and the book of Acts paint a vivid picture of this unforgettable man, and as we read, we get to know him better than any other disciple. From his first contact with Jesus Christ, it was clear that he would not only be a disciple but that he would be discipled by Christ Himself, his abilities refined through fellowship and failure. The Lord called this capable, confident fisherman to Himself and then patiently transformed him into a God-dependent leader.

Simon Peter was introduced to Christ by his brother, Andrew. Certain that Jesus was the Messiah, Andrew found his brother and "brought him to Jesus" (John 1:42). At this first meeting, Jesus announced, "Thou art Simon the son of Jona," and then promptly changed Simon's name to "Cephas, which is by interpretation, a stone." Andrew was probably surprised by that choice, for he knew that his brother was not a rock but a volatile, impulsive man instead. Jesus had plans to transform Peter's temperament until he was as steady as a stone. The process of change would be painful, but that day, Jesus saw Peter not as he was but as he someday would be.

After his unusual introduction to Jesus, Peter apparently

went back to his regular job for about a year. The next time we meet him, he's tending his fishing nets by the lake of Gennesaret (Galilee). He and his partners had thrown their nets all night into the shallow waters where the fish usually gathered but had caught nothing.

1. Read Luke 5:1–11. What sort of physical and mental condition would those fishermen have been in that morning?

_____

What did Jesus ask them to do?

_____

How did Peter respond?

_____

Throwing nets into deep water during the daytime was not reasonable, especially after an exhausting, unproductive night, and at the direction of a carpenter, not a fisherman. But Peter did what Jesus asked. Soon the nets were filled to breaking, loading the ships to the point of sinking.

2. How did Peter's spirit shift from verse 5 to verse 8?

_____

What traits are present in a man who reacts like that?

_____

_____

3. Now Peter comprehended that Jesus was much more than just a teacher. What had Jesus just done that only God can do?

_____

4. And once more, Jesus told Peter's future. What would Peter do from now on (verse 10)?

_____

What do you think that means?

_____

5. Peter and the others did not hesitate. They immediately "forsook all and followed him" (verse 11). List some of the things they were leaving behind.

_____

_____

_____

Would you find that easy? We know Peter as a man who was quick to acknowledge and repent of his sinfulness and a man passionate enough about Christ to leave all to follow Him. Peter became part of the inner circle of disciples and the leader among them.

6. What traits of Peter are revealed in these passages?

Mark 1:35–37

_____

Matthew 16:21–23

_____

Matthew 17:1–4

_____

John 13:1–9

_____

Peter was bold, confident, enthusiastic, courageous, spontaneous, frank, energetic, vigorous, and strong! I love to be around people like that; they invigorate me! But Peter also had some of the "flip side" qualities that go along with these: he was volatile, impulsive, unpredictable, hot-tempered, brash, hasty, and impetuous. He was a major overreactor, and the other disciples never knew what he'd do next. (He didn't either!) Yet he possessed this rare and valuable trait: he had genuine faith in Jesus Christ. He was a true and passionate believer.

PETER'S FAITH

7. Read Matthew 14:22–33. What was Peter's response to seeing Jesus walking on the Sea of Galilee?

Peter acted just the way we would expect, leaping out of the boat to get to Jesus! It's easy to criticize the doubt, fear, and focus on the storm that caused him to sink. But don't ignore this: Peter is the only human being who has ever walked on water. If that's "little faith" (verse 31), what would the Lord would call your faith?

8. Read John 6:66–69. Why didn't Peter do what many of the other disciples did?

I love Peter's logic! Simple faith—like a child's—is the strongest. Peter boldly confessed his faith in Christ about six months before the crucifixion (Matthew 16:13–17). Jesus had just asked His disciples, "Whom do men say that I the Son of man am?" Some had speculated that Jesus was one of the dead prophets come back to life, but Jesus wanted to know what His closest companions believed. He asked, "But you, who do you say that I am?" Peter, true to form, spoke for the whole group. And he said a mouthful—a mouthful of truth!

Thou art . . .

- the Christ [the Messiah, the anointed One],

- the Son [the second member of the Trinity],
- of the living God [the eternal One, Jehovah].
- (Matthew 16:16)

9. How did Peter know this? Was this just his reasoned opinion (verse 17)?

In the next verse, Jesus says that those words from the mouth of Peter (*petros*—a small stone) would become the *petra* (foundation stone) of His church. The truth contained in his confession is the bedrock of our Christian faith. The prediction Jesus made at their first meeting was being fulfilled. Peter would soon be steady as a stone—though his path to stability would lead through failure.

PETER'S FAILURE

10. Jesus tried to warn His vulnerable disciple. During the Last Supper, when He announced that He was going away alone, Peter objected. How did he try to convince Jesus that he should be allowed to go with Him (John 13:36–38)?

What was Jesus' gentle warning to Peter?

What would you have done if Jesus had predicted that about you? Begged the Lord to protect you from the temptation? Sealed your mouth with duct tape? Locked yourself in a closet until noon? Not our friend Peter!

11. Read a parallel passage in Matthew 26:33–35. What was Peter's response to Jesus' warning?

Overconfidence is a dangerous trait, and Peter had more than his share. Maybe he thought self-control could negate Jesus' prophecy—that he knew better than the Lord how he would act. Before any of us pass judgment on Peter, maybe we should consider how we respond to warnings. How do you react to teaching about the dangers of the internet, movies, and television? Do you think that counsel to avoid the world's music and entertainment is out of date? Does teaching about dressing modestly and acting with discretion seem unnecessary? Maybe you believe that such cautions are important for others, but not for you—you can handle it! Peter's story is a warning against any sort of self-reliance.

> Wherefore let him that thinketh he standeth take heed lest he fall. (1 Corinthians 10:12)

> He who thinks himself so much stronger than his brethren, is the very man who will prove to be weaker than any of them.

> Charles H. Spurgeon

12. Self-trust is always unwise, for you have a powerful enemy who wants to make you a spiritual casualty. Jesus had just warned Peter about Satan (Luke 22:31–32). What did the Wicked One want to do to Peter?

_____

What was Jesus' prayer for Peter (verse 32)?

_____

What did Jesus see in Peter's future?

_____

The word *you* in verse 31 is plural. Satan had already succeeded with Judas, and now he wanted to make traitors of the rest of the disciples. He wants you too. But he cannot come near you without the Savior's permission. Whenever He does allow Satan to shoot his fiery darts your way, He prays for you as He prayed for Peter, for He wants to use your trials, and even your failures, to fortify your faith. How loving Jesus was to warn Peter, and us. And how sweet to think that when He sees us under attack, He prays for us.

Peter was blinded by reckless self-confidence. It might have helped if he had prayed with Jesus in the Garden of Gethsemane, but he didn't. He slept instead (Matthew 26:40–43). There is no doubt that Peter sincerely loved the Master, for when Judas showed up leading a crowd from the chief priests armed with swords and sticks, Peter pulled out a sword and cut off the high priest's servant's ear (John 18:1–11). I suspect he wasn't aiming for an ear!

It's hard to know whether we should admire Peter's zealous defense of Jesus against a hostile crowd (at least he did *something*) or to laugh at the notion that the Son of God needed the protection of one small sword.

13. Why did Jesus tell Peter to put away his weapon (John 18:11; Matthew 26:52–54)?

_____

Christ had surrendered to the cross, so He submitted calmly to arrest. The terrified disciples ran away, except for two—Peter and John. John entered the high priest's palace with Jesus while Peter remained in the courtyard. Read these four Gospel narratives to get a full picture of this sad story that followed:
- Matthew 26:69–75
- Mark 14:66–72
- Luke 22:54–62
- John 18:15–18, 25–27

14. What was Peter's response to each accusation?

_____

15. What does only Matthew record about Peter's language (Matthew 26:72)?

_____

16. Why do you think Peter was so frantic to deny that he knew Jesus?

_____

17. Four things happened at the same moment (Luke 22:60–61). What were they?

_____

_____

_____

Until this horrible night, Peter had been a vigorous disciple of Jesus Christ. But at the worst possible moment, during the Lord's illegal trial, Peter denied Him. He never expected that his curses would be heard by Jesus Himself. Pictures have been painted of the moment when "the Lord turned, and looked upon Peter" (Luke 22:61).

18. If you were an artist, how would you paint Jesus' face at that moment?

_____

What do you think His expression communicated to Peter?

_____

19. In the middle of the mob, Jesus' eyes met Peter's as though they were the only two present. What happened next reveals the depths of Peter's heart. What did he do (Luke 22:62)?

_____

Why did Jesus allow Peter to fail? Why does He ever let those who sincerely love Him deny Him by their words, actions, or silence? He has a purpose for failure. When handled properly (repented of and forgiven), failure can be one of God's most useful tools to forge godly character.

Failure Crushes Pride

> Pride goeth before destruction, and an haughty
> spirit before a fall. (Proverbs 16:18)

Pride is always, always a predictor of failure. The more certain you are that you will not fail, the more certainly you will. On the other hand, the humbling that results from failure can make you more likely to succeed.

> Before destruction the heart of man is haughty,
> and before honour is humility. (Proverbs 18:12)

Peter's awareness of his failure sent him rushing into the night, fleeing from Jesus' gaze, sobbing in repentance. That doesn't sound like the Peter we have come to know. He'd never slunk away before! He was already a different man. His tears softened the proud soil in his heart. From then on, he would know what he was capable of and would be on guard against his flesh and the Devil.

20. Read the words he later wrote to other believers in 1 Peter 5:5–9. Which of his instructions reflect lessons he learned through failure?

_____

_____

_____

Jesus allowed Peter to be sifted as wheat (Luke 22:31). This is not the sort of sifting of flour you're familiar with. It's a winnowing process, the tossing of grain in a bowl that allows the breeze to blow away the chaff (hulls, dust) and leave behind only the good grain. The Lord let Satan "shake up" Peter through this failure, and as a result, much fleshly self-reliance was filtered from his character.

Failure Strengthens Our Bond with the Lord

> The Lord is nigh unto them that are of a broken
> heart; and saveth such as be of a contrite spirit.
> (Psalm 34:18)

Peter had been as close as any human being to Jesus, but Jesus had had to talk loud and straight to get his attention—and even then, Peter often promptly forgot what he'd heard. But now all it took was one look from the Savior and Peter got the message. Failure granted him a new intimacy and sensitivity to Christ. Just as a shepherd often carries a lamb with a broken leg, Jesus carries a broken but repentant Christian close to His heart, creating new bonds of love and dependence as He whispers, "I love you. I still love you. I have hope for you even if you have none for yourself."

21. How did the resurrected Jesus encourage Peter (Mark 16:5–7; Luke 24:33–34; 1 Corinthians 15:3–5)? (Remember that Cephas is another name for Peter.)

_____

_____

_____

Peter soon took his place again among the disciples. After the resurrection, he fished with six others on the Sea of Galilee. When Jesus appeared on the shore with a picnic breakfast, Peter didn't hide in shame but instead was eager to be near the One Who had forgiven him.

22. How can you tell that though he was now different in character, he still had the same vivid personality (John 21:7)?

_____

Your temperament will not change as you grow spiritually, but God will polish its strengths and refine its weaknesses. Make every effort to be like Jesus Christ, but never try to copy anyone else's personality. God made you the special, unique person you are, for His purpose and His glory, so be yourself!

Failure Prepares Us for Success

People who have failed and repented have unique strengths. One is that they are less likely to fall again. You will behave differently once you have learned that failure can happen to you. Those who have failed and repented also find their experience an effective tool for ministry. They are quick to compassionately warn those about to fall into the same ditch and are among the first on the scene to help pull them out. Peter, after he was converted, strengthened his brethren, as Jesus had prayed (Luke 22:32). He led a ten-day prayer and business meeting of 120 believers and preached a powerful message on the Day of Pentecost.

23. What happened after that sermon (Acts 2:37–41)?

_____

Jesus had been crucified during the Passover celebration; Pentecost came fifty days later. That means that only seven weeks passed between Peter's failure and his restoration to such amazing usefulness! When you repent, forgiveness is immediate (1 John 1:9). Full restoration, though, is not instant, and rarely is it as rapid as it was for Peter. In fact, there are some sins from which a fallen believer can never fully recover. But for Peter, Pentecost marked the beginning of decades of powerful ministry. Through God's power, he healed the sick, raised Dorcas from the dead, boldly challenged unbelievers, took the lead in church councils, and was miraculously delivered from prison. Late in life, he authored the two epistles in the New Testament that are named for him. Church history records that he was martyred by being hung upside down on a cross, pleading that he was not worthy to be crucified in the same way as Jesus. Peter was a thoroughly changed man!

Failures aren't good in themselves. But God can work them together for your good. If you have failed, don't despair. Repent and begin again! But never forget what you are capable of, and use your experience to help others. Deal directly but gently with those who fail and repent, forgiving and encouraging them. That is what Jesus did—and He is our example.

The hour of crucifixion had come. Jesus had been mocked, scourged, and tortured. Soldiers had pressed a crown of spiky thorns onto His head and forced Him to carry His own cross. Now they hammered spikes into His hands and feet and lifted the cross upright so all could witness His horrible death.

Some who loved Jesus had followed Him to Golgotha. They stood in the crowd watching as He agonized and bled, thinking about what He had said about His kingdom and the power given Him by His Father. Surely, they thought, He won't let the Romans get away with treating Him like this. He's just waiting for the right moment to call legions of angels to His rescue. Soon He'll come down from that cross in triumph, destroy His enemies, and set Himself on their throne! Any minute now, they must have thought—any minute now, He'll show them!

But He didn't. Jesus stayed on the cross until He breathed His last breath. When a soldier stabbed a spear into His side, water and blood came out—sure proof of death. Jesus was dead. Absolutely, unmistakably dead. His friends were stunned. Their anguish at His death was compounded by their shock that He had not done what they had expected Him to do.

> And all the people that came together to that sight, beholding the things which were done, smote their breasts, and returned. And all his acquaintance, and the women that followed him from Galilee, stood afar off, beholding these things. (Luke 23:48–49)

103

MISUNDERSTANDINGS

Not even His closest circle of friends had understood Jesus' predictions of His death, burial, and resurrection. They didn't comprehend that His kingdom was spiritual, not political. Jesus had tried to explain it to them and to prepare them for what was coming. His first prediction of His future came just after He had cleansed the temple, which He called "my Father's house" (John 2:16). The disciples recognized His zeal for the purity of the temple as an attribute of the Messiah, but the temple authorities, who did not believe in Him, challenged Him to prove that He had authority to do what He had done. "What sign shewest thou unto us, seeing that thou doest these things?" they asked (verse 18).

1. What proof did Jesus offer them (John 2:19)?

_____

2. What did the Jews think He meant (verse 20)?

_____

According to verse 21, what temple was He actually referring to?

_____

Jesus was even more direct with His followers in Luke 9:18–22. Peter had confessed his belief in Jesus as "the Christ of God" (the promised Messiah). Jesus then told them what was coming for the Messiah.

3. What four specific predictions did He make (verse 22)?

_____

_____

_____

_____

4. On His final journey to Jerusalem, Jesus reviewed with the disciples the hardships the Scriptures said the Messiah must endure. These were very specific. Read Luke 18:31–34. Who would His persecutors be?

_____

What sufferings would come to Him?

_____

_____

And then what miracle?

_____

But the disciples still didn't get it. Peter, in fact, "took him, and began to rebuke him, saying, Be it far from thee, Lord: this shall not be unto thee" (Matthew 16:22). Even after the resurrection, the disciples were steadfast in their insistence that Jesus' kingdom would be on earth, asking if the time had come for Him to "restore again the kingdom to Israel" (Acts 1:6). They knew that the Messiah would be the King of Kings—but they did not understand that He first had to be the suffering Savior.

MISGIVINGS

Since the disciples had misunderstood, they grieved His death in bewilderment. Mingled with their sorrow was terror that the Jewish and Roman authorities would come after them next, for they were the accomplices of a crucified criminal. Remembering Judas, they probably wondered, even as they hid out together, who else in their little group was a traitor. Then they heard the astonishing news from Mary Magdalene that she had seen and spoken to the risen Lord. Peter and John also saw that Jesus' body had vanished but did not comprehend what had happened.

5. Why did the disciples not understand (John 20:9)?

_____

After Mary Magdalene and her companions met two angels who reminded them that Jesus had predicted His death and resurrection (Luke 24:4–9), these jubilant women ran to the huddled apostles with their good news.

6. Why did the men not believe them (Luke 24:11)?

_____

_____

_____

WITHDRAWAL

It must have been terribly frustrating for the women to have their glorious news treated as nonsense! (You may have experienced the same sort of rejection when you've excitedly shared the gospel.) Other followers of Jesus also doubted the reports of His resurrection. We meet two of them in Luke 24:13–53.

7. Where were they going?

_____

How long was the walk?

_____

That's about seven and a half miles. It's likely that these were both men. One had the masculine Greek name Cleopas (verse 18). Verse 13 says that they were traveling "that same day."

8. What day was it?

_____

What a time to be leaving Jerusalem! On that day, in that

place, God had fulfilled the promise of the ages. Satan's defeat was guaranteed; the power of death was broken; the sacrifice for sin was made; the work of redemption was accomplished. Oblivious to the thrilling victory Almighty God had just won over sin and death, these two disciples focused instead on their own loss and trudged down the road toward home. Discouraged, disappointed, and disillusioned, as they walked they were talking it through, hashing it out, trying to figure out what had gone wrong. If the road to Emmaus had a gutter, these two gloomy guys were in it.

> And it came to pass, that while they communed together and reasoned, Jesus himself drew near, and went with them. (Luke 24:15)

9. It was not unusual for travelers to connect for safety or conversation as they walked a lonely road. Why do you think they didn't recognize Jesus when He joined them (verse 16)?

_____

Either He had been transfigured in some way or their sight was affected so that He looked different. This was a supernatural occurrence, for they knew Jesus well.

COMMUNICATION

10. Jesus noticed their emotional state. How did they feel (verse 17)?

_____

Cleopas was astonished that their travel companion did not know what had just happened in Jerusalem. How could He not have heard the news that everyone had been talking about? Of course He did know. He had been the main character!

11. Why then do you think He asked them to tell Him?

_____

The One Who "knoweth what things ye have need of, before ye ask him" (Matthew 6:8) still says, "in everything . . . let your requests be made known unto God" (Philippians 4:6). He wants you to talk to Him every moment (1 Thessalonians 5:17), to communicate with Him continuously (Romans 12:12), and to pray always (Ephesians 6:18).

12. Why does He want you to tell Him about everything all the time, when He already knows it?

What does this tell you about the relationship God longs to have with you—especially when you are discouraged?

13. It must have been a relief to be able to pour out their troubled hearts. In simple, earnest words, they told their tale to this sympathetic stranger. Read Luke 24:19–21. Who had they believed Jesus was, and what had they expected Him to do?

Notice that they did not call Him "Messiah." Maybe His death had caused them to doubt His truthfulness—even His identity. For a disciple, that is the essence of discouragement. An Emmaus road is any place of disappointment with God, of dissatisfaction with His provision, of discontentment with His providence. Women have different ways of traveling that miserable road. Some eat. Some shop, figuring that if they buy something new, they'll feel better. "God didn't satisfy me, so I'll find some other way to be satisfied," they say by their choices, forgetting that only He "satisfieth the longing soul, and filleth the hungry soul with goodness" (Psalm 107:9).

Maybe you don't max out your credit cards or eat an entire cheesecake when you are disappointed with God, but instead you complain to anyone you can drag along the road with you. You dump your frustrations on your husband; on your mother, sister, or best friend; on your pastor's wife; on your next door neighbor; or even on a stranger in the grocery checkout line. These kind folks listen patiently and try to help. They "commune and reason" with you, sympathizing and empathizing, but usually are unable to change your circumstances. They often just end up in the gutter too, for it's much easier to pull someone down into your ditch than for them to lift you out. When you're on an Emmaus road, you need much more than human sympathy. You need what Jesus offered His disciples that day: the Scriptures. What a privilege they had—to hear the Word expound His Word!

COMFORT

14. What Scriptures did Jesus guide them to, and what did He point out there (Luke 24:26–27)?

_____

_____

These may have been some of the Old Testament prophecies Jesus used:

Genesis 3:15—The Messiah will suffer, but Satan will be destroyed.

Numbers 21:8–9—Salvation will come through looking in faith at one "lifted up" (see John 3:14–15).

Jonah 1:17—The Son of man would spend "three days and nights in the heart of the earth" as Jonah was "in the belly of the fish" (see Matthew 12:40).

Zechariah 12:10–11—There will be "great mourning in Jerusalem" when its "inhabitants . . . shall look upon me whom they have pierced."

15. What details of Christ's suffering and crucifixion were prophesied long ago in these passages?

Psalm 22:1–18

Psalm 69:19–21

Isaiah 53:3–7

When Jesus died on the cross, some thought His death proved He was not the Messiah. But in reality, His death proved that He was! Jesus soon went through this same exercise with His other disciples. "Then opened he their understanding, that they might understand the Scriptures" (Luke 24:45).

16. Which Scriptures did He use (verse 44)?

17. When Jesus called the two disciples "fools" (verse 25), it was not a term of contempt but implied instead that they were thoughtless or unthinking. What were they "slow of heart to believe"?

Their slowness was understandable. These disciples were caught up in the values of a world that admired the power of emperors and their armies. They could not imagine a kingdom in which the last would be first and where the path to life moved through death. To them, thrones were to be built in marble palaces, not in human hearts. The kingdom of God is still a mystery to many.

18. What truths did Jesus make sure His followers understood (verses 46–48)?

Jesus did not give His disciples new truth. He helped them understand and apply what they already knew. Can you think of times when an old, familiar passage from the Bible became a brand new friend to you? That often happens during times of trial and discouragement. Bible words you've read a thousand times before suddenly begin to shine on the page!

This walk-along Bible study must have brought the two disciples comfort and joy because when the travelers reached their village and Jesus indicated that He would keep traveling, they "constrained Him" to stay overnight. I wouldn't have wanted Him to leave either! He had shown them that the upsetting events in Jerusalem were simply part of God's good plan for the ages—a plan made long, long ago. His teaching method was simple: He pointed them to His written Word. It's obvious that those two disciples needed a teacher. We do, too. We are as slow to learn and as quick to forget as they were, so our Father, a few weeks later at Pentecost, sent a Teacher to "abide with [us] forever" (John 14:16).

19. Who is He, and what are His assignments (John 14:26; 15:26; 16:13)?

_____

_____

_____

When the trio of travelers arrived in Emmaus, the sun was low, and Jesus agreed to stay with them. "And it came to pass, as he sat at meat with them, he took bread, and blessed it, and brake, and gave to them" (Luke 24:30). A simple meal—an ordinary scene—but with one great difference: the One breaking the bread was the Bread of Life. As He broke it, the disciples' eyes were opened, and they suddenly recognized Him.

While wandering through a large art gallery, I came across a painting of this moment in Luke 24. In the picture, three men sat at a rough table, holding broken loaves of bread. The center figure was serene, but the others were not! They were staring wide-eyed across the table—shocked, amazed, astounded. I am as helpless to describe their astonished expressions as I am to paint a picture like that. It stirred my soul, and for a long time I sat on a gallery bench staring, trying to imagine what it would have been like to suddenly know that their supper guest was the living Son of God. Someday, we too will see the resurrected Christ face to face. What a day that will be!

TRANSFORMATION

20. What happened at the same instant they realized Who their Guest was (verse 31)?

_____

Jesus rose bodily from the grave, but His glorified body was different. It passed through linen grave wrappings and closed doors (John 20:19, 26). He was not a ghost, for He ate broiled fish and a honeycomb (Luke 24:42–43) and invited Thomas and others to touch the nail prints in His hands and the wound in His side (John 20:27; Luke 24:40). Jesus took pains to prove to the disciples that He was no apparition: "Behold my hands and my feet, that it is I myself: handle me, and see; for a spirit hath not flesh and bones, as ye see me have" (Luke 24:39).

21. The instant Jesus disappeared, the two disciples exclaimed, "We should have known all along Who He was!" Why did they say that (verse 32)?

_____

That phrase literally means that their hearts were set on fire. Not only were their hearts kindled—their feet must have been, too, for though it had been a stressful, exhausting day, they "rose up the same hour, and returned to Jerusalem" (verse 33). That was another seven-and-a-half-mile trip through the night, but I suspect they made it in record time. This news couldn't keep!

Can you imagine the scene? They burst in, panting, before

the quavering disciples, crying, "He's alive! He's alive! We saw Him! He walked with us! He talked to us! He ate bread with us! He's alive!" Then suddenly Jesus Himself appeared to prove their message true. He was alive, and He was there with them. His coming banished all discouragement from the room (verses 33–36).

When Jesus wanted to help His two discouraged disciples, He did not change their circumstances. Instead, He guided them to see those circumstances in the light of God's good, eternal plan— and that changed everything. He will do the same for you. If you are walking down an Emmaus road right now, look beside you. The perfect Helper is there, waiting for you to turn to Him. Listen as He opens His Word to you. Your heart will burn, and your discouragement will vanish.

> Whom have I in heaven but thee? and there is none upon earth that I desire beside thee. My flesh and my heart faileth, but God is the strength of my heart, and my portion forever. (Psalm 73:25–26)

LESSON 11

Some trials are just inconveniences, but others are wretched ordeals. During heavy trials, you may feel isolated, thinking that no one else can possibly understand your pain. But because of the incarnation, Jesus understands! While living on earth, He experienced the entire scope of human experience—including trials. In this lesson, we will go with Him into the Garden of Gethsemane and learn how to handle our trials as He handled His.

As Jesus neared the end of His life on earth, His rejection was almost complete. Isaiah's prophecy was coming true:

> He is despised and rejected of men; a man of
> sorrows, and acquainted with grief: and we hid
> as it were our faces from him; he was despised,
> and we esteemed him not. (Isaiah 53:3)

Just before His crucifixion, Jesus and His disciples celebrated the Passover. Immediately after sharing bread with Jesus, Judas went out into the darkness to betray Him. Then Jesus announced to the rest of the group that He was about to leave them. They would be scattered, He said, and Peter would deny even knowing Him. Jesus gave them final instructions and promises as they walked together to the Garden of Gethsemane, where they had often rested and prayed among the olive trees.

But tonight there would be no rest for the Savior. The hour He had often spoken of was almost here—the hour for Him to "fall into the ground and die" (John 12:24). "The Lamb slain from the foundation of the world" (Revelation 13:8) had assured His disciples that all that would happen would come by His own permission: "I lay down my life. . . . No one takes it from me" (John 10:17–18). Though He knew what was coming and was willing to endure it, conflict still raged in the serenity of Gethsemane that night, as Jesus wrestled in prayer.

115

Many artists and songwriters have depicted this prayer for us, and their descriptions usually show a hushed and tranquil scene, with the light from heaven falling upon a kneeling Savior, his hands clasped devoutly in front, his eyes cast heavenward, and his lips moving faintly as he prays his "cup of suffering" prayer. All is silent, subdued, and serene. But this is not the biblical account at all. The careful student can almost hear the shrieks of demons and the crackling flames which filled the gentle Garden of Gethsemane that awful night.

—Unknown

Carefully read Matthew 26:36–46; Mark 14:32–42; and Luke 22:39–46. Compare these accounts to discover the sequence of events in Gethsemane. "Stay awake and pray with me" was all Jesus asked of His friends. This is a touching moment in the life of our Savior, as for the first time, He directly asked for their help and support. Instead of giving it, they fell asleep, leaving Him alone.

SHRINKING FROM SUFFERING

1. It is in Gethsemane that we most clearly see the union of the human and the divine in the incarnate Son of God. How is He described in Mark 14:33?

Jesus knew terror as He looked into the impending storm. As God, Jesus could foresee the horrors; as man, He shrank from them. As man, Jesus was learning from His sufferings (Hebrews 5:8), and what He learned makes it possible for Him to identify with our pain.

You and I have often felt the "twisted gut" that comes when we have done wrong, the uneasy feeling that makes it hard to rest until we have been forgiven. Imagine all the guilt of all the people who have lived and ever will live loaded all at once onto One Who had never experienced guilt for even one sin. He was about to bear the crushing weight of all our sin "in his own body on the tree" (1 Peter 2:24). The cup He was about to drink was overflowing with all the wickedness of the world. Imagine being asked to plunge into sewage, to be submerged in a stinking, putrid tank of filth—out of love for people who would not love you in return—and you may come to some small understanding of what Jesus did for us.

> For he hath made him to be sin for us, who knew
> no sin; that we might be made the righteousness
> of God in him. (2 Corinthians 5:21)

2. Foreseeing the pain ahead brought Jesus to a point in His flesh that few experience. What physical detail of His suffering does Luke record in Luke 22:44?

Jesus had hematidrosis, a rare condition that causes a person under severe stress (such as facing death) to sweat blood. Jesus was battling with the Devil and his army of demons, who were making a radical attempt to murder Him in the garden before He could reach the cross.

SORROW OF SEPARATION

3. Because of Gethsemane, Jesus understands sorrow. How did He describe His emotions (Matthew 26:37–38)?

He was "very heavy," in a torment of suffering, overwhelmed by sorrow. "This word is used by the Greeks to denote the most extreme anguish which the soul can feel—excruciating anxiety and torture of spirit".[1] Though it was late and the disciples had already had a traumatic day, it is still a wonder to me that those sleepyheads were not startled into wakefulness when He told them that the anxiety and grief engulfing Him were severe enough to cause His death. The impending physical sufferings of the cross were dreadful enough, but Jesus also knew that while on the cross, He would be separated from His Father. Jesus never for a moment ceased being God the Son—the Father's own image, beloved and well-pleasing to Him—but when the Father looked at the cross, He saw not His Son but sin personified.

> Surely he hath borne our griefs, and carried our sorrows. . . . He was wounded for our transgressions, he was bruised for our iniquities: the chastisement of our peace was upon him; and with his stripes we are healed. . . . The Lord hath laid on him the iniquity of us all. (Isaiah 53:4–6)

The Father and Son had known perfect unity since eternity. But now the Father turned away from Him, for on the cross, the innocent Jesus *became sin*. He became hatred, murder, lust, fornication, gossip, theft, lying, cursing, gluttony, embezzlement, addiction, molestation, drunkenness, hypocrisy, pornography, bribery, false worship, religious pride, unbelief . . .

The Lamb, our substitute sacrifice, was where you and I deserve to be, and God's anger toward our sin was directed toward Him. He was our Passover Lamb, "sacrificed for us" (1 Corinthians 5:7). The physical and spiritual agonies of the cross reveal both how much God hates sin and how much He loves sinners. To save our lost souls, the Father was "pleased . . . to bruise him; he hath put him to grief" (Isaiah 53:5, 10).

Separation of the Son from the Father was an essential part of the plan of redemption. But the temporary estrangement of Calvary broke Jesus' heart. Darkness covered the heavens as Jesus reached the peak of His sufferings.

4. "About the ninth hour Jesus cried out with a loud voice."
   What did He say (Matthew 27:46)?

_____

But the Father did not answer. He did not—could not—rescue the Son. The Trinity's plan of redemption had to be carried out, even at the cost of directing the Father's justified wrath toward sin onto His sinless, only begotten One, even to the point of enduring an unbearable separation from Him. If you die without receiving the pardon for sin that the cross made possible, you will experience in hell the agony of eternal alienation from God. But if by grace through faith your sins have been forgiven, rejoice in this: Jesus has already endured sin's penalty for you. You will never for a single second—in this life or in the next—be separated from Him!

5. Read Romans 8:35–39. List the things that cannot separate us from our Savior.

_____

_____

_____

    Can you think of any being, power, or event not included in that list?

_____

    Some of us think at times that we could cry, "My God, my God, why hast Thou forsaken me?" There are seasons when the brightness of our Father's smile is eclipsed by clouds and darkness; but let us remember that God never does really forsake us. It is only a seeming forsaking with us, but in Christ's case it was a real forsaking. We grieve at a little withdrawal of our Father's love; but the real turning away of God's face from His Son, who shall calculate how deep the agony which it caused Him?

                                  –Charles H. Spurgeon

6. Maybe at some point in a heavy trial, someone has told you that a Christian should not weep when in pain, that grieving is a sign of a lack of faith. How do you know it is not sinful to cry when you're in pain and sorrow when your heart aches?

_____

SYMPATHY FOR US

> For even hereunto were ye called: because Christ
> also suffered for us, leaving us an example, that
> ye should follow His steps. (1 Peter 2:21)

Because of Gethsemane, Jesus Christ can understand our sufferings. But Jesus doesn't only understand pain; He showed us by His example how to handle it. In Mark 14:35–36, Jesus laid down a five-step path for us to follow through trials.

Step 1—Go to the right source for help—"He went forward a little, and fell on the ground, and prayed"

Jesus left His closest friends to go to His Father for help. Kneeling, or perhaps prostrate with His face on the ground, He prayed aloud. The disciples heard a few of His words, but for at least an hour (interrupted by His checking on them), He groaned in fervent prayer.

What an example for us. Who do you dial first when a problem comes up? Does that person always answer the phone? Even if he or she does answer, has time to listen, and sincerely tries to understand and help, often it's beyond his or her ability to give you a lasting solution. How long is it before you remember to pray? Are you prone to look in the wrong direction for help?

7. What are you supposed to pray about (Philippians 4:6)?

_____

8. How many of your troubles are you supposed to give to Him (1 Peter 5:7)?

_____

> Trust in him at all times; ye people, pour out
> your heart before him: God is a refuge for us.
> Selah. (Psalm 62:8)

Step 2—Come on the basis of your relationship—"Abba, Father"

In the Garden of Gethsemane, Jesus used the Aramaic name "Abba" for His Father (Mark 14:36). It's the only time recorded in the Gospels that Jesus used this tender and familiar name that children used for their daddies, an intimate name reserved for family use. My husband has called each of our three children by special nicknames since they were tiny. Though they are now adults, I still hear him use those names, especially when they are troubled. Using a sweet family name immediately reminds both father and child of their relationship—of who they are to each other. "I know who you are," the name says. "You're mine, and I love you."

9. Why do you think Jesus chose to use that name for His Father at this moment?

_____

I don't want you to use (or know!) our private nicknames. They are just for family. But the amazing fact is that you are not just allowed, but invited, to call the heavenly Father "Abba," just as Jesus did.

10. On what basis are you allowed to use that name (Romans 8:15)?

_____

11. Which member of the Trinity makes this possible (Romans 8:16; Galatians 4:6)?

_____

When you are hurting, come to God as the most loving, devoted Father you can imagine. "Like as a father pitieth his children, so the Lord pitieth them that fear him. For he knoweth our frame; he remembereth that we are dust" (Psalm 103:13–14). He longs to know every need and share every sorrow. You never need to present a false face to Him. Reverently but candidly express every feeling and fear (after all, He already knows them all!).

12. Read Psalm 77 aloud, and you'll hear Asaph communicating some strong emotions to Jehovah during trouble. List some that speak to you personally.

_____

_____

_____

13. In Psalm 88, the writer is so full of grief, so desperately sorrowful, that he seems on the brink of complete despair. He brings that misery to God without pretense or reservation. What desperate emotions pour out of his heart?

_____

You may never have felt this low, but even if you do, Jesus understands.

> Deep depression of spirit is the most grievous of all trials; all besides is as nothing. . . . Humbly adore the King of glory as having once been brought far lower, in mental distress and inward anguish, than any one among us; and mark His fitness to become a faithful High Priest, who can be touched with a feeling of our infirmities. . . . Let us not give way to despair, since through this dark room the Master has passed before us. Our souls may sometimes long and faint, and thirst even to anguish, to behold the light of the Lord's countenance: at such times let us stay ourselves with the sweet fact of the sympathy of our great High Priest.
>
> _–Charles H. Spurgeon_

Step 3—Plead the power of God—"All things are possible unto thee"

14. What can happen when God goes to work for you (Matthew 19:26)?

_____

15. What is too difficult for Him (Jeremiah 32:17, 27)?

_____

16. How much can He do (Ephesians 3:20)?

_____

> Thine, O Lord, is the greatness, and the power,
> and the glory, and the victory, and the majesty:
> for all that is in the heaven and in the earth is
> thine; thine is the kingdom, O Lord, and thou art
> exalted as head above all. (1 Chronicles 29:11)

Think of the power the incarnate Lord showed on earth! He controlled nature, stopping storms and walking on water. He healed lepers and those lame from birth, gave sight to the blind and hearing to the deaf. He saved the adulterous and demon-possessed, thieves and publicans. He produced money from a fish's mouth and food for thousands from one little boy's lunch bag. He is still the same, and He can deliver you from your trial. He has power over all the circumstances of your life, just as He had control over the events in Gethsemane.

> When the chief priests, temple officers, and elders came to the Garden of Gethsemane to arrest Jesus, they succeeded only because a sovereign God permitted them to succeed. . . . Who allowed them the power to capture Him? It was God, without Whose leave not even a sparrow can fall to the ground. God is omnipotent, never slumbering, just, righteous, and forever in control. He was not taken by surprise. All was working then, as it is always working, into a pattern for good.
>
> Our own difficulties often appear to be random. Our tragedies look wildly uncontrolled. They are not. They are _subject_. Limits are set. God is quietly at work, standing in the shadows, ceaselessly watching over His children.
>
> —_Elisabeth Elliot_

123

Jesus' prayer assumed that the Father could take away the coming trial on the cross and save sinners in some other way, that He could have let the cup pass without His Son touching it if He chose. During a mission trip to Africa, my husband and several others were invited to visit the home of a powerful local chief. The chief offered water to his guests—drinking from the glass first and then passing it to the others in turn. Dave had been very careful not to drink the local water for fear of disease, but not wanting to offend, he decided to just go ahead and drink it and trust the Lord. The glass moved from the chief to his assistant, to several African believers who each took a sip, and then on to the local missionary—who deliberately drank all that was left. The cup passed from my husband that day, but it didn't pass from our Lord. The cup can pass from you if the Lord chooses. Jesus prayed for deliverance on the basis of the unlimited power of God, and so can you.

Step 4—Make a simple, direct request—"Take away this cup from me"

Jesus' request was straightforward: He asked the Father to spare Him the cup holding the wages of sin. Sometimes a woman in trial will find her prayers all muddled—jumbled, tangled, and blended with worried thoughts. A friend of mine was once so troubled about a family need that instead of praying coherently, she was just blubbering to the Lord, when He seemed to ask her directly: "What is it that you want Me to do?"

When you are in too much pain to speak or even think rationally, write down your basic request of God. Then even when your emotions are overwhelmed, your prayers can still have focus and direction—and you'll recognize the answer when it comes! When Jesus encountered people who needed a miracle, He sometimes posed a question like the one He asked the blind beggar Bartimaeus: "What wilt thou that I should do unto thee?" (Mark 10:51). The answer was obvious: the blind man needed sight! But Jesus seemed to delight in knowing what it was He was being asked to do and then doing precisely that.

17. What trial is wringing your heart right now? Write down a concise answer to Jesus' question "What do you want Me to do?"

_____

_____

Step 5—Submit to the will of the Father—"Nevertheless, not what I will, but what thou wilt"

Nevertheless is a big word in more ways than one. Jesus had asked His Father for deliverance, but now He said, "Nevertheless, I cling to no will of My own in conflict with Your will. I am resolutely submitted to You. In joyful obedience, I will drink the bitter cup that comes from Your hand." There never was any conflict between the will of the Father and that of the Son. Submission to the will of God, even in a painful trial, is the spirit Jesus modeled for us.

18. When is it hardest to take this fifth step, to pray "Thy will be done"?

_____

19. What happened near the end of Jesus' prayer (Luke 22:43)?

_____

Heaven is with you, too, when you writhe in pain. God sees and knows, and He will send the comfort you need, including this great consolation: He understands. Because of the incarnation, He knows all about trials. When you walk through pain, follow His footsteps. He is the God of Gethsemane, and He is with you when you hurt.

God is never the source of temptation to sin, but He allows it, as He does all things, for our good.

> Blessed is the man that endureth temptation: for when he is tried, he shall receive the crown of life, which the Lord hath promised to them that love him. Let no man say when he is tempted, I am tempted of God: for God cannot be tempted with evil, neither tempteth he any man. (James 1:12–13)

> The Lord knoweth how to deliver the godly out of temptations. (2 Peter 2:9)

Jesus understands our struggle with sin, for while living on earth, He also was tempted. His battle with sin was worse than anything we could imagine. We fight against the world, our flesh, and demons, but Jesus "came face to face with the prince of the power of the air, with the god of this world, with Lucifer, son of the morning, fallen from his high estate of the first rank of heaven, and now leader of the hosts of darkness."

–G. Campbell Morgan

Read Matthew 4:1–11, Mark 1:12–13, and Luke 4:1–13 for an overview of the temptation in the wilderness, which came at the beginning of Jesus' public ministry. Satan was ruthless in this opening skirmish, for he knew that if he could get Jesus to sin even once, he would have won the battle of the ages. With even one stain on His record, Jesus could not be the Lamb "without blemish and without spot" required for redemption (1 Peter 1:19). There could be no salvation through the death of a sinless Savior, and Satan would have averted his own doom. But Jesus did not give

127

in! He defeated the enemy. If you follow His example in your own battles with the Devil, you can win too.

THE PURPOSES OF TEMPTATION

1. Jesus endured temptation in order to be your perfect example. The lures the Devil cast at Him were much like the ones he uses on you. In how many ways was the Lord tempted (Hebrews 4:15)?

   _____

2. Jesus also faced temptation so that He could be your helper. What can He do for you (Hebrews 2:17–18)?

   _____

3. If God doesn't want you to sin, why does He let you be tempted (Deuteronomy 8:1–3)?

   _____

When you fail the test of temptation, you are humbled. Failure can make you a more useful, God-dependent servant (as it did for Peter). When you have victory, you strengthen your spiritual muscles, and the next battle is easier to win. By choosing God's way when you're tempted to choose your own, you prove that you love Him more than you love yourself. And that gives Him glory!

THE PERMISSION FOR TEMPTATION

4. Why did Jesus go into the wilderness (Luke 4:1)?

   _____

During a recent cross-country drive, I stared across the Arizona desert and tried to imagine a forty-day stay in that wilderness without water, food, or shelter, under unrelenting satanic assault. To attempt anything like that without supernatural sustenance, without the unmistakable leading of the Holy Spirit, would be just plain stupid. In the same way, it's presumptuous to walk deliberately into temptation and then expect God to deliver you from it.

> Enter not into the path of the wicked, and go
> not in the way of evil men. Avoid it, pass not
> by it, turn from it, and pass away. (Proverbs
> 4:14–15)

If you're trying to lose weight, don't visit the chocolate shop. If you need to watch less television, don't buy one with a bigger screen. If you are determined to avoid gossip, stay away from people who gossip. Whenever you see temptation approaching, run the other way! And as you run, look for the way of escape. It will always be there.

> There hath no temptation taken you but such
> as is common to man: but God is faithful, who
> will not suffer you to be tempted above that ye
> are able; but will with the temptation also make
> a way to escape, that ye may be able to bear it.
> (1 Corinthians 10:13)

When in God's providence you find yourself under a barrage of heavy temptation, you can be sure God knows about it and is there to help you, for any tempting of His child requires His consent. Job's story illustrates this. God allowed heavy trials to end Job's remarkable prosperity, and then He gave Satan permission to use those trials as a means to entice Job to sin.

5. Read Job 1:6–12. What did Satan hope to accomplish by taking away Job's prosperity?

_____

What limit did God set on what Satan could do to Job?

_____

How did Job respond to the temptation that came with his trials (1:20–22)?

_____

6. Job's wife became a tool of temptation when she urged Job to do just what Satan hoped he'd do. What was Job's response to her urging (Job 2:7–10)?

_____

_____

_____

Job's sufferings and temptations eventually ended. Jesus' wilderness experience ended after forty days, when Satan departed from Him "for a season"—until another opportune time (Luke 4:13).

7. God has set a limit for your temptations too. What is it (1 Corinthians 10:13)?

_____

Temptation is not designed to make you fail or to give you an excuse to sin. Instead, it is an opportunity for you to find the way of escape, to glorify God by defeating Satan. Even if you're asked to face the same level of physical pain, economic loss, or bereavement as Job, to the point that you're tempted—as Job's wife advised him—to "curse God and die" (Job 2:9), you can have the kind of confident faith that caused Job to say in his pain, "I know that my redeemer liveth, and that he shall stand at the latter day upon the earth: and though after my skin worms destroy this body, yet in my flesh shall I see God" (Job 19:25–26). Like Job, you can't see what is going on in heaven, but you can be sure of this—Satan cannot touch you without the permission of your Father.

THE TIMING OF TEMPTATION

After a Spiritual Victory

The prologue to Christ's wilderness temptation was His baptism. About age thirty He came from Galilee to the Jordan to be baptized by John (Matthew 3:13). This was His presentation as Messiah and the beginning of His public ministry.

8. Read Luke 3:21–22. What was Jesus doing as He was baptized?

_____

We're not told what He said, but I think that Jesus may have been promising His Father that He would do His will—that He would complete the work He had been sent to do. As He was praying, suddenly "the heaven was opened," and the two other members of the Trinity made their presence known.

9. What (Who) was the visible sign of Jesus' anointing and empowering to do His work?

_____

Who was the audible witness to Jesus' deity?

_____

"You are My Son, My Beloved. In You I take delight!" the Father said. What a moment! God the Father confirmed that Jesus was His Son, and the Spirit showed that He would empower Jesus' work. You'd think that Satan would have been intimidated by those heavenly announcements—but he wasn't deterred in the least. Instead he quickly launched an all-out assault on the Savior.

Jesus' reign as Prince of Peace opened with a battle against the prince of this world.

10. How quickly did the wilderness temptation follow Jesus' baptism (Mark 1:12)?

_____

131

Luke even links the two events in one sentence: "And Jesus being full of the Holy Ghost returned from Jordan, and was led by the Spirit into the wilderness, being forty days tempted of the devil" (Luke 4:1–2). Temptation immediately after spiritual victory is common. Baptism was a peak experience for Jesus, and remembering the Father's words of love and praise surely encouraged Him when He stood toe to toe with the Devil. A sweet time with God may be His way of getting you, too, ready to enter a wilderness.

There is another reason God may allow the Devil to attack right after a spiritual victory. The mighty prophet Elijah was at the peak of his ministry. Through him, Jehovah had just exhibited His astounding power to wicked Ahab and all the people of the land through two amazing miracles (1 Kings 18:21–46). But then a trial came in the form of Jezebel's threats.

11. While coping with this trial, what was Elijah tempted to do (1 Kings 19:1–4)?

_____

Read verses 5–18. What was God teaching Elijah?

_____

_____

_____

Right after a spiritual victory, be on your guard, for that's when Satan will return with a vengeance. Recalling that victory will help you "quench the fiery darts of the wicked" (Ephesians 6:16). Stand firm, and as you do, look for the lessons that the Lord is teaching you. He may be allowing you to go through a temptation to keep you from trusting in your own strength or your own experience rather than in your Savior's power to deliver.

When You Are Vulnerable

We aren't told where the wilderness was, but it was probably the region between Jerusalem and the Dead Sea, near where John had been preaching and baptizing (Mark 1:4–5). It was wild, barren, and bleak—an utterly desolate and solitary place.

12. Jesus was alone in the wilderness, except for what companions (Mark 1:13)?

_____

Those critters were kept from harming their Creator—but their prowling and threatening didn't make the days any more pleasant! Angels arrived at the end of the forty days (Matthew 4:11). The Devil was there the whole time (Luke 4:2). It seems likely that Jesus experienced a variety of temptations during His six weeks' fast and that the three specific temptations we read about came near the end, as His hunger, thirst, and loneliness increased.

Satan did not spare Jesus in His weakness. And he never gives you a break either. There's no sympathy in Satan, no consideration for your weakness. He will never say, "She's tired and pressured, so I'll give her a break today," or "She has a headache, so I'll leave her alone for a while." He will tempt you more, not less, when you are vulnerable, so watch out for his wily ways when your usual defenses are down.

13. What special temptations come to you when you are

Alone?

_____

Tired?

_____

Sick?

_____

Hungry?

_____

Rushed?

_____

Around irritating people?

_____

Pressures like these make it easier to fall into sin. But even in wonderful surroundings, perfectly well and rested, among ideal companions, temptation can still arrive. Adam and Eve lived in a perfect place with "every tree that [was] pleasant to the sight, and good for food" (Genesis 2:9) and with God as their companion, but they still didn't resist the serpent's enticement to eat the one fruit they were denied. The first time they were tempted, they gave in. Jesus, on the other hand, in a wasteland without any food or a single friend, successfully endured Satan's attacks for almost six weeks. He knew how to conquer temptation! Let's see how He did it and learn from His example.

VICTORY OVER TEMPTATION

The First Temptation

14. What did Satan ask Jesus to do (Matthew 4:3)?

_____

_____

Satan knew Jesus was the Son of God, for he had just heard it announced from heaven. Why then would he say, "If you are the Son of God . . ." (verses 3, 6)?

_____

15. Why do you think he chose food as his first tool of temptation?

_____

I can picture Satan picking up several large, smooth stones and offering them to Jesus, knowing that Jesus could instantly transform them into fresh, delicious loaves of bread. He wasn't asking Jesus to gorge Himself on a huge meal but just to eat a bit of bread. And eating is not a sin. Why would it have been sinful for Jesus to do as Satan suggested?

16. Why did Jesus refuse to supply His own food (Matthew 4:4)?

_____

This verse refers to the time when the children of Israel were complaining that God had led them into the wilderness to starve (Exodus 16:1–28). How did God feed them?

_____

When He gave the Israelites detailed instructions about gathering manna (Exodus 16:4, 28), what was He testing?

_____

What did He want them to learn (Deuteronomy 8:1–3)?

_____

17. When you resist the temptation to complain about your circumstances and wait obediently for God to provide your manna, you prove something wonderful! What is it (John 14:21, 1 John 5:3)?

_____

Jesus set an example of obedience by refusing to supply His own needs, in His own time, in His own way.

> [Satan] bids the Lord prove his Sonship by catering for himself; and yet that would have been the surest way to prove that he was not the Son of God. A true son will not doubt his father, and undertake to provide his own bread; he will wait to be fed by his father's hand. The evil one would have the only-begotten Son cease to depend on God, and take matters into his own hands.
>
> *-Charles Spurgeon*

18. Satan wanted Jesus to meet a legitimate need in the wrong way. He's still using this tool of temptation. What otherwise valid physical desires do people satisfy in sinful ways?

_____

Which "lust of the flesh" (1 John 2:16) is a particular problem for you?

_____

Jesus chose a verse perfectly suited to counter His specific temptation. What Scripture can you use in your own battle?

_____

The Second Temptation

You may have noticed that Matthew and Luke reverse the order of the last two temptations. We will follow Matthew's sequence.

19. Where did the Devil take Jesus (Matthew 4:5–6)?

_____

What did he ask Jesus to do?

_____

The Holy Spirit had led Jesus into the wilderness. Now Satan led Jesus to a pinnacle of the Jerusalem temple, perhaps one that overlooked the Kidron Valley from a height of about 450 feet. As they stood there, Satan quoted from Psalm 91, a song full of assurances of God's sovereign protection of His children.

20. Which verses of that psalm did the Devil recite?

_____

> The Devil knows and uses the Bible. But he "utterly twisted its meaning, employing a passage about trusting God to justify testing Him."[2]

Watch out for people who quote the Bible to excuse sin. False teachers bait their hooks with of a tiny bit of truth. Just because Scripture is used doesn't mean that truth is being taught. Make it your goal to know the Word of God so well that you can quickly tell when it's being used as a tool to spread lies.

Suppose Jesus had stepped off that pinnacle and glided down onto the ground unharmed. People would have been astounded! They may have fallen at His feet and worshiped Him. He deserved their worship, but the time for that had not yet arrived. Satan's suggestion was contrary to the will of the Father, and that is what Jesus was committed to do.

> For I came down from heaven, not to do mine own will, but the will of him that sent me. (John 6:38)

In this temptation, Satan was insinuating that Jesus needed to test God's promises, as though He might not be trustworthy. In answer, Jesus again quoted from Deuteronomy.

21. What was His answer (Matthew 4:7)?

_____

_____

_____

Jesus was not willing to put on trial the God Who cannot lie (Titus 1:2).

> It is when we doubt a person that we make experiments to discover how far he is to be trusted. To make experiments of any kind with God, is to reveal the fact that one is not quite sure of Him.

> *–G. Campbell Morgan*

Have you ever been tempted to doubt God or His Word? Are you ever tempted to put God to a petulant test, saying, "If You're really up there, then . . ."? God is honored most by those who "walk by faith, not by sight" (2 Corinthians 5:7) and believe even when they cannot see (John 20:29).

> Whom having not seen, ye love; in whom, though now ye see him not, yet believing, ye rejoice with joy unspeakable and full of glory. (1 Peter 1:8)

The Third Temptation

22. Where did Satan next take Jesus (Matthew 4:8)?

_____

What did he show Him?

_____

What exchange did Satan propose?

_____

This was probably a vision, for Luke says that Satan showed Jesus "all the kingdoms of the world in a moment of time" (Luke 4:5).

Did Satan have authority to make this offer? In Luke 4:6, he claimed that he did, "All this power will I give thee, and the glory of them: for that is delivered unto me; and to whomsoever I will I give it." Jesus didn't deny the power of Satan in this world.

23. What did He call him in John 12:31, 14:30, and 16:11?

_____

24. There's little doubt that the Devil has immeasurable influence over politics and world affairs. What did Paul call him in 2 Corinthians 4:4?

_____

Notice in that verse what Satan does to his subjects. No wonder he has so much power over those who "believe not." But if you are a believer, your eyes are open to the truth—God is the ruler of our universe! Though the whole world "lieth in wickedness," we are His children, and though the wicked one can tempt us, he cannot touch us (1 John 5:18). Since we are not Satan's children, he has no authority over us (1 John 3:10).

Sometimes when our little dog Max was in the backyard, the neighbor's children would call, "Here, Maxie, Maxie, Maxie!" Often he'd run to them, because they usually had a doggie treat for him. I never tried to teach him to obey their voices, but I worked hard to train him to come when I called. (He never did, but I really did try!). He wasn't obligated to obey anyone but his master. And you have no obligation to heed Satan's call. You can disregard any "treats" he holds out to you and delight in obeying God instead.

The third was the most blatant of the temptations. The other two were proposals that did not violate the clear commands of God, but this one did. Satan suggested a shortcut to glory that bypassed the cross and echoed the wicked desire that led to his fall from heaven (Isaiah 14:12–14).

25. In response, Jesus again quoted from Deuteronomy. What command did He quote (Deuteronomy 6:13–14)?

_____

_____

Jesus had endured enough. He called the wicked tempter by name for the first time (Satan, or "Adversary") and gave him an order (Matthew 4:10). "Away with you!" He commanded, and Satan left, for even the arrogant god of this world must obey the One before Whom someday "every knee should bow, of things in heaven, and things in earth, and things under the earth" (Philippians 2:10). The Devil left Jesus for a while, but he would be back. And he will always come back to tempt you too. Just as Satan left, angels arrived to comfort the exhausted, hungry Savior, and perhaps to celebrate His victory! I think they likely do the same for you when you win your battles with sin.

> Are they [angels] not all ministering spirits, sent
> forth to minister for them who shall be heirs of
> salvation? (Hebrews 1:14)

Temptation is agonizing, for the Devil is malicious. It's continual, for he is persistent. But temptation is a conflict you can win if you will follow your incarnate Savior's battle plan.

Watch out for the enemy.

> Be sober, be vigilant; because your adversary the
> devil, as a roaring lion, walketh about, seeking
> whom he may devour. (1 Peter 5:8)

Be aware of his sneaky tactics.

> Lest Satan should get an advantage of us: for we
> are not ignorant of his devices. (2 Corinthians
> 2:11)

Use God's Word as your best defense.

> Stand therefore, having your loins girt about
> with truth. (Ephesians 6:14)

Don't give in. You don't have to!

> Submit yourselves therefore to God. Resist the
> devil, and he will flee from you. (James 4:7)